Organization and Management of IT

Volker Johanning

Organization and Management of IT

The New Role of IT and the CIO in Digital Transformation

 Springer

Volker Johanning
Marl am Dümmersee, Germany

ISBN 978-3-658-39571-1   ISBN 978-3-658-39572-8   (eBook)
https://doi.org/10.1007/978-3-658-39572-8

This Springer imprint is published by the registered company Springer Fachmedien Wiesbaden GmbH, part of Springer Nature.
The registered company address is: Abraham-Lincoln-Str. 46, 65189 Wiesbaden, Germany

Paper in this product is recyclable.

Preface

What is the Purpose of IT Organizations in an Enterprise?

How must IT organizations be structured to efficiently and effectively fulfill their purpose?

What role does IT and its chief CIO need to play in the company in order to be successful?

What are the truly purposeful leadership maxims in the highly dynamic digital age?

What roles and personnel profiles does an IT organization need in order to hold its own in tomorrow's digital competition?

These are the central questions answered in this book.

However, in order for IT to fulfill its purpose in the company, it is not enough to simply set up a new IT organization. The new constructs must be consistently implemented through new management approaches and instruments of IT. This book therefore pursues the approach of rewriting the role of IT in the company, building appropriate organizational models and governance structures, and living these through leadership in the company in such a way that IT exchanges its pure service provider role for that of an active shaper. This new role is a strategic competitive factor for companies, because in many, if not most, companies, the business models are now based on IT.

This means that IT is increasingly becoming the heart of the company. The CIO is called upon to take on the role of shaper and continue to assume responsibility at the first level of the board and management.

However, such organizational adjustments or reorganizations are true change challenges. No other project is as directly and obviously about new roles, tasks, and positions as a reorganization. Therefore, such a project is a real Herculean task for those responsible. And when tasks in the newly created IT organization are outsourced to external service providers, the project has reached its peak. It could hardly be more demanding. But at the same time it is fun to see how something new grows, how old problems suddenly vanish into thin air, and how IT gains in reputation and takes on a new role as a shaper. Therefore, this path is always and definitely worthwhile!

However, it should be pointed out at this point that constant reorganizations paralyze and are no longer taken seriously. Therefore, the so-called "organisitis" should be avoided.

Only a one-time and well-executed organizational change followed by time to take a deep breath after the big change can be successful. The new organization must be allowed to arrive, must be able to settle, and can only create stable conditions in the company over time. People in organizations can certainly cope with change and transformation, but they also need periods of calm and stability to ensure productive performance.

Furthermore, it should be said that there is no perfect organization. All organizations require compromises and have their advantages and disadvantages. The pure theory of organizational theory does not resonate in practice, and it will always be nearly impossible to create and implement the optimal organization. However, speaking with Malik [1] and Drucker [2], there are four specific requirements for organizations that also apply to IT organizations in particular:

1. Clear focus on the customer, i.e., the business goals and the business bottlenecks that need to be solved by IT.
2. Create an organization which ensures that employees – both IT and business – can actually do their jobs.
3. Leadership of knowledge workers can only happen at eye level. It is empowerment and under no circumstances instruction or correction in the traditional command and control style from the Taylor era.
4. Meaning and purpose are crucial: IT organizations need a clear vision and a goal. The question of "why" must not only be answered top-down, but by the entire organization and be able to support it.

The book in front of you gives you a very practical guide to organizational change or reorganization of IT with many tips on change management, leadership, and agile methods and approaches in the new IT organization.

The maxim is: carry out the change of the organization very conscientiously, with a lot of patience, very good planning, and sensitivity, and observe the four requirements mentioned above. Only then will it be successful and only be on the agenda again in a few years instead of leading to constant reorganizations.

Sincerely yours,

Marl at the Lake Dümmer   Volker Johanning
Dümmer, Germany
Winter 2020

References

[1] *Malik, Fredmund*: Führen Leisten Leben, 6. Auflage, Campus Verlag, 2006.
[2] *Drucker, Peter F.*: "Management's New Paradigm", http://www.mit.edu/~mbarker/ideas/drucker.html, MIT, abgerufen am 30.12.2019.

Contents

Part I

Introduction: The IT Organization Over Time

Organizations in General

1

Abstract

This introductory chapter first deals with the general definition of the term "organization" in the company. It then looks at the historical and organizational development of IT – from its timid beginnings as an organizational department with huge computing machines to IT in today's digital age. This historical classification of IT is important in order to understand the opinions and (pre)judgments toward an IT organization that are often still prevalent today, because this understanding is the basis for the transformation of IT from a machine room to a shaper and innovator.

1.1 Definition of Terms

Where does the term "organization" come from, and when did it first become common to use it for structuring and managing business operations?

Already at the beginning of industrialization in the early nineteenth century, the division of labor in manufacturing became so complex that it had to be regulated, i.e., organized. In this context, "organizing" means "creating structures" [1].

It is important to realize that structures in companies are not only created to tame complexity but above all to support the company's strategy. "Structure follows strategy" is the well-known basic rule for this, according to which the organization is to be designed in such a way that the corporate strategy is supported in the best possible way.

Since the organization follows the strategy and in many companies today the strategic guidelines are subject to constant market pressure, this has an impact on the organization, because this is not constant, but subject to constant change. Therefore, many

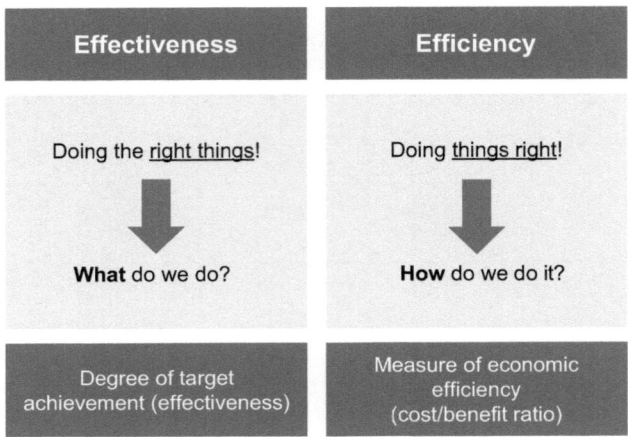

Fig. 1.1 Effectiveness versus efficiency

organizational structures in companies have often "grown historically" and are not so much subject to a conscious design process [1].

In the context of the broader definition of the term "organization," a differentiation between **organizational structure** and **process organization** is of great importance. The organizational structure regulates the delineation of tasks, competencies, and subordinate relationships, which in practice result in an organizational chart. Typical questions in relation to the organizational structure are "What is to be done?" and "Who does what?". However, when it comes to the question of "What is to be done when and in what order?", this refers to the process organization. This regulates the internal processes within a company, the so-called business processes, and is today often simply called process management.

In this framework, the two concepts of effectiveness and efficiency also play a role.

As can be seen in Fig. 1.1, efficiency stands for "doing things right" and effectiveness for "doing the right things." Both are needed to organize complex corporate constructs, such as the IT organization, and to make them manageable.

1.2   Organizations Today

Many companies today are exposed to very strong market pressure. Deliveries are made every minute due to state-of-the-art IT, and information flows constantly and can be accessed by anyone from anywhere at any time. How does this change not only our lives in general but also the way we work and thus the way organizations are designed in the company?

Author Niels Pfläging has examined this phenomenon in more detail in his book *Organization for Complexity*. He sees a fundamental difference in the way work looks today compared to when organizations were created: the industrial age. Pfläging describes three ages with the so-called Taylor tub (see Fig. 1.2):

- The manufacturing age with high dynamics based on local markets and high customization (until approx. 1850/1900).
- The industrial age with low dynamics, almost inertia, based on wide markets with little competition (from 1850/1900 to approx. 1970).
- Today's knowledge age, which is characterized by very high dynamics on global markets.

What is exciting about Pfläging is the transition between the industrial age and the knowledge age. Between 1990 and today, so much has happened due to major upheavals such as the Internet, globalization, and completely new communication possibilities that companies from the industrial age did not really know how to react and in some cases still do not know how to react today. Suddenly, completely new competitors have emerged and are emerging virtually out of nowhere, which can also pose a threat to large companies and corporations – the dinosaurs of the industrial age. Just remember the completely new competitors in retail (keyword "Zalando") or the completely new competitor in the car market (Google has already proven autonomous driving).

What are the means of choice for companies that still follow old-fashioned rules of organization and management from the times of the division of labor of Taylorism?

One reorganization follows the next. Added to this are cost-cutting programs. In the industrial age, it was customary to first take a break after a reorganization. The new

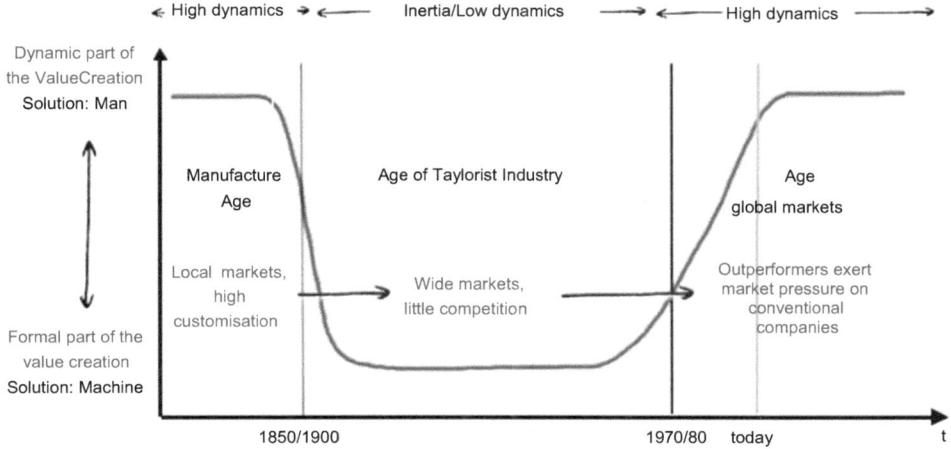

The dominance of high dynamics and complexity is neither good nor bad. It is a historical fact.

Fig. 1.2 The Taylor trough

organization was supposed to "settle down," and each member of the organization had time to find his or her new role, to shape it, and thus to see the interfaces in the company slowly grow and function. Today, however, things have to work immediately, and if they don't, the next reorganization sometimes follows right away. It is expected that results are visible immediately; otherwise, the shareholders threaten to sell the shares, and this in turn can mean the sudden loss of jobs for managers. The pressure on the old-fashioned, Tayloristic organizational thinking has become huge and leads to constant change in the form of reorganizations. This seems to be the only way out. But how do companies have to organize themselves in the knowledge age, and what role does IT play in this?

Reference

1. *Capgemini*: "IT-Trends 2019", https://www.capgemini.com/de-de/wp-content/uploads/sites/5/2019/02/IT-Trends-Studie-2019.pdf, abgerufen am 28.12.2019.

2

Abstract

IT in particular, as the driver of the knowledge age in companies, plays a virtually pre-destined role in shaping an organization in times of high dynamics with global markets. This chapter therefore takes a closer look at where IT comes from, what role IT plays today, and what its future role may be.

2.1 From the Beginnings of IT to 2010

In the early days, IT – usually referred to as "EDP" – was also responsible for the topic of organization. This was reflected in organizational names such as "EDV/ORG" or "organization and EDP." There was even the role and position of "organizer."

But in order to understand how this came about, one must take a closer look at the beginnings of IT. In their book *Erfolgsrezepte für CIOs (Recipes for Success for CIOs)*, Brenner and Witte have mapped the historical development of IT in companies (see Fig. 2.1). This illustration is very important for understanding the role of IT and the CIO (chief information officer) in companies today. This is because, according to Brenner and Witte, the historical development of IT has made it so deeply ingrained in the minds of those responsible in the business departments and the company management that the CIO and IT are "machinists" instead of "shapers" [1].

In a very abbreviated manner, but looking at the core of the question of the development of IT, the following summarizes the time periods of IT shown in Fig. 2.1 (based on [1]):

The **1950s** were the starting point for IT. The starting point was highly complex calculations in the military sector, which could only be carried out with the help of computer technology. More and more, IT was also used in the civilian sector in the mid-1950s. Pure

V. Johanning, *Organization and Management of IT*,
https://doi.org/10.1007/978-3-658-39572-8_2

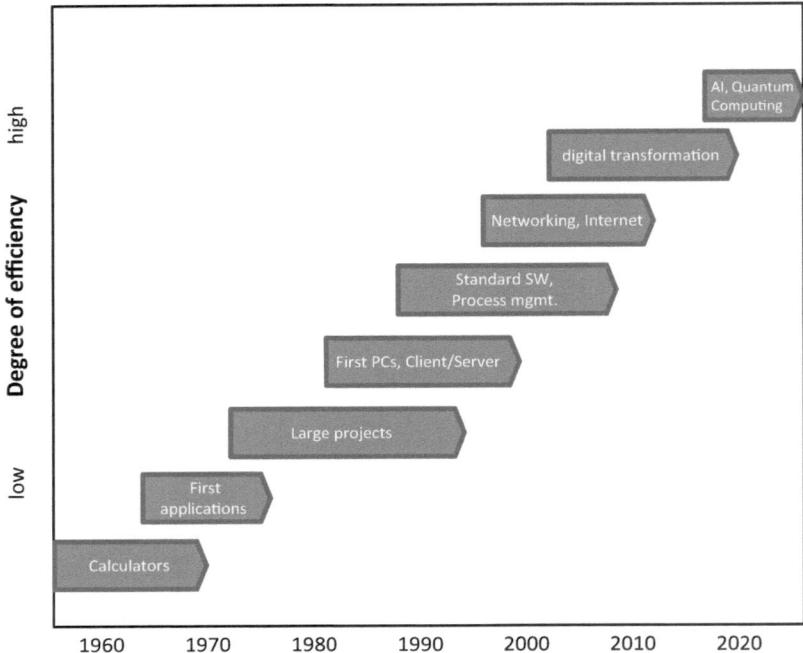

Fig. 2.1   The historical development of IT

technicians (often physicists or electrical engineers, because computer scientists did not even exist back then) made sure that the huge machines in companies could perform difficult calculations. Applications or even apps, as we know them today, did not yet exist. Hardware was supplied, and programs had to be written at the system level, which then executed certain functions.

In the **1960s**, IT continued to develop in the direction of mass data processing. The economy flourished after World War II, and especially mail order companies, banks, and insurance companies benefited from IT due to the processing of large amounts of data that had become possible. It is important to remember that this type of data processing was not possible for every single user. This is because there were no personal computers or terminals for every employee; instead, the result of data processing was presented in the form of punched cards on paper. One has to imagine it in such a way that only selected technicians had access to the emerging computer centers. These brought their self-created programs there and had – sometimes only days later – their results back in the form of punched cards. The first major application of EDP at that time was the automation of accounting processes. Therefore, the EDP manager was also subordinate to the head of finance. And that is also the reason why even today – 50 years later – many CIOs report to the CFO! However, the IT manager had a very prestigious job back then. He was highly respected for getting a grip on these huge machines in the completely new and respect-inspiring data centers.

The **1970s** were marked by a shift toward applications. The focus was no longer on hardware alone but increasingly on applications. There was a shift from processing data in batch mode to real-time systems. This meant that you no longer had to wait a night or whole days for the results of the computers but got results directly and in real time on monitors and no longer just on punch cards. This was also the time when IT projects first saw the light of day. The requirements of the departments grew as it was recognized that there was a lot of potential in IT. Project management was the method of choice, but – as is still painfully known today – deadlines could often not be met, budgets got out of hand, and in the end, one was happy if at least half of the requirements could be implemented. Unlike today, however, the confidence in this new technology was so great that people forgave mistakes and saw them as an unavoidable learning process. The importance of EDP and the EDP manager increased more and more, and in many cases, he made a career in the company. The dependency on EDP became greater and greater. Nevertheless, the EDP people were regarded as experts who pursued a kind of secret science with abstract concepts and devices. The typical anglicisms and abbreviations from the EDP world were very foreign to the conventional managers and employees from the specialist departments. The image of the well-paid but non-business-oriented computer scientist became entrenched.

In the **1980s,** personal computer (PC) made its way into companies. The mere fact that word processing software replaced the electric typewriter was somewhat revolutionary. However, the new PCs were initially an enormous burden for IT managers and were sometimes even seen as a danger. Until then, the EDP department with its computer center could determine which application would run for whom. Now, all of a sudden, the departments were able to buy their own applications, and there was a "proliferation" that no longer seemed to be controllable. Many applications were bought several times, the data sovereignty of the EDP was lost, and everyone stored data locally on his PC, which was no longer available for others. Accordingly, they were often available twice or several times in the company and sometimes even in different versions. The maintenance and further development of applications that could suddenly be developed by the departments themselves became impossible and led to a strict rejection of PCs by the EDP managers. Their sovereignty over the EDP was in danger, but PCs were becoming cheaper and more user-friendly, so that the EDP could not defend itself against the mass distribution of PCs at every workplace. In addition, new players established themselves in the IT market who understood that the separation of PC and server made a new form of data storage for several applications simultaneously possible and necessary. First and foremost, we should mention Oracle, which, along with IBM with its DB2 product, very quickly advanced to become the leader of a completely new database market. SAP AG, founded in the 1970s, also joined this market. By integrating and linking all the functions of business administration on the basis of a database, an application had emerged that possessed enormous automation and simplification advantages for companies. By the mid- to late 1980s at the latest, most IT managers had realized that the triumphant advance of the new PC and server technologies was unstoppable. They subordinated themselves to this dictum, and departments were created that were no longer called EDP, but information management. These departments were no longer primarily concerned with technology, but with data modeling, information management, and the implementation of applications that were no longer written in-house but had to be purchased from major players such as SAP and Oracle and integrated and implemented in the company.

The **1990s** were the age of processes and standard software. Until the end of the 1980s, the organizations of companies were adapted to the applications. As a result, many isolated solutions were created, and each department had its own organization and processes, mostly separate from the others. At MIT in Boston, people thought about developing a view of the organization that spanned processes and departments. This led to a process-oriented business design called "business process reengineering." With the help of consultants, many companies began to analyze and redesign their processes. However, this highly customized remodeling of the process landscape was extremely complex. And when applications had to be developed for precisely these individual processes, it quickly became apparent that this undertaking not only seemed unaffordable but also downright impossible. This was the hour of the standard applications, first and foremost the so-called ERP systems such as SAP. This was because this standard software already had process models that roughly fitted most companies. They were mainly introduced in the administrative areas such as finance and accounting as well as human resources standard applications. As a result, companies again adapted to the applications. The only exceptions were special processes, which were adapted or, in the technical jargon, "customized" in their application by the providers of the standard software, in some cases with a great deal of effort and expense. The role of the "organizers" no longer existed, and so the responsibility for the introduction of this standard software and thus also the design of the workflows, the processes, and the organization in the company often went to IT and into the hands of the CIO. The departments, however, sometimes strongly resisted this and wanted to retain responsibility for their own processes and procedures. This led to IT taking responsibility for the introduction of standard applications, but the issue of process optimization or the design of processes and workflows was often not clearly defined. The "IT people" were considered too technical, which is why they were not trusted to design the processes and procedures of the entire company. The business departments, for their part, had great respect for difficult and, from their point of view, incomprehensible and complex system implementations and sometimes deliberately stayed out of it in order to blame IT and the CIO afterward for unsuccessful implementations. Today, people talk about change projects and change management, but the problem still does not seem to have been solved optimally.

The **2000s** were marked by networking and the Internet. This meant that processes and products were to be transformed into the new world of the Internet. Virtual marketplaces for the exchange of goods emerged, and electronic business was on everyone's lips and led to data and information being available across the globe from 1 s to the next. This has revolutionized many industries, most notably retail, which has been transformed from brick-and-mortar stores to electronic online shopping outlets. Amazon and Zalando are typical examples of this. Even bank branches no longer need a multitude of employees on-site, because banking transactions are now conducted online for the very most part. The Internet has found its way to every consumer through the introduction of the iPhone and the subsequent variety of smartphones or tablets. No matter where and at what time, access to the Internet and thus to knowledge, information, and data is possible constantly and everywhere. What does this mean for IT in companies? In the early days of the Internet, its potential was recognized by some progressive business leaders. This led to new companies being formed or new departments being created to deal with the issue of using the Internet. Consultants were hired to create new business models and adapt existing business models to the Internet age. However, those who were mostly not asked were the CIO and his colleagues from IT. IT was still seen as being stuck in the technology corner, the introduction of standard software in the previous decade had not always been to everyone's satisfaction either, and therefore hardly any CIO or IT department was given the chance to play a shaping role in the company when it came to the Internet. Another big issue of this decade was the possibility to map processes not only within the company and its departments but also even across companies. All of a sudden, the entire value chain of a company came into focus due to the fast and global Internet: From the supplier to the end customer, a digital artery could supply everyone with the necessary data. This further optimized existing business models, for example, by allowing suppliers to take over warehousing and deliver to the second; the end customer then knew at all times when his product would reach him. In these developments, too, IT took over the technical part, but the idea, the conceptual design, and the associated creative role lay in the specialist departments.

Between **2010** and **2015**, the topic of "digitalization" had then banished its way. Networking through the Internet entered a new era. Ever-improving infrastructure ensured faster connections and meant that IT technology could be used almost anywhere in the world at any time.

Many terms characterize the world of digitalization, Big Data, cloud, IoT (the Internet of Things), Smart Industry, M2M (machine-to-machine communication), and artificial intelligence, which is on the rise. What all these terms have in common is that they originate from IT and are essentially further developments of the historical development of IT shown.

Now, at the latest, even the last person will realize that IT has created the transition from the industrial age with assembly line work to a true information and knowledge society.

2.2   Where Does IT Stand Today?

If you look at the development of IT over the decades just outlined, it is particularly notice-able that the role and perception of IT got stuck somewhere in the 1990s and early 2000s. IT has been able to stomp its way out of the penalty corner of being too expensive and purely technical until today to the role of designer.

Today, it is still the case in many companies that the day-to-day work of IT is character-ized by the introduction of standard software and its customizing as it was in the 1990s. And it is still the same questions about responsibility for the design of the organization and processes that seem to remain unresolved.

However, there is now the so-called cloud, via which software can be obtained anytime and anywhere. The cloud pioneer Salesforce, for example, has now brought this concept to such a mature stage that it is quite easy to operate Salesforce and adapt it to individual needs, which is why the business department does it itself in most cases. IT usually does not notice this at all. Because there is no longer any need for an in-house server, and even the settings, customizing and administration of users can be organized and carried out by anyone in the department.

This means that IT itself has meanwhile lost its very own task of providing technology or is in the process of losing it. In the past, it was not trusted with the task of design, and now it is also losing its very own role as a machine operator, as Brenner and Witte put it.

At first glance, this seems to herald the demise of the IT department. But perhaps it is also an opportunity to finally put IT in perspective or a plea for the creation of a new role for IT and that of the CIO.

What Are IT Managers Doing to Avoid This Dilemma?
If you look at the literature on IT management topics, you will notice that it mainly deals with the design of the governance function as well as the optimization of process functions of IT. Countless best-practice approaches have emerged over the last 15 years, which are now standard in larger IT organizations.

These include, above all, the standardization of service management processes with the help of ITIL, but also the so-called COBIT processes for the design of the governance function. The optimization of IT processes has cost a lot of time and energy in recent years. The result is optimal processes within the IT organization. But what about the inter-faces to the business department? Has the recognition of IT within the company increased as a result? Can customer problems really be solved here? Has IT gained in importance as a result and already been able to take on the role of designer?

Often, the result of optimizing the process functions within the IT organization's own boundaries is unfortunately so unsatisfactory that the departments and the customers turn away even further. After all, tickets from anonymous e-mails and highly standardized hot-lines that only answer standard inquiries and cannot help otherwise are not exactly customer-friendly. Even worse are the IT processes in the so-called change and request management, when this has been standardized to such an extent that customer requests are irrelevant and IT itself dictates when new changes are to be implemented or when a request is to be accepted as a requirement by the business department and when not.

It is no wonder that the business departments are resigned and no longer want to discuss with IT how things could be done better. The CIO or IT manager has demanded these standardizations because the IT system landscape has become so complex and thus hardly controllable. He also had no other choice because standardization in this fast-paced world has advanced to the point where IT can no longer keep up with the ever-changing demands on IT systems. So was the optimization and standardization of IT processes wrong, or did they just overtighten the screw a bit? These are questions that are very topical today and cannot be answered with the help of further optimization of the process organization alone.

Now it is a matter of rethinking IT, redesigning the organizational structure of IT in the company, and, above all, designing a new role for IT in the company. Looking at the IT organization alone is not enough: The perspective must be broadened. The requirements of the business departments and IT must be looked at from the company's point of view – from a bird's-eye view, as it were. How should the company be structured so that IT can become active as a shaper, in part acting as a specialist department itself, and in addition keeping the technology running as a commodity?

Reference

1. *AXELOS/TSO (The Stationery Office)*: "ITIL Foundation, ITIL v4", 1. Auflage, AXELOS/ TSO 2019.

Part II

The Structure of IT Organizations

The Organizational Structure of IT: Various Models in Pro and Contra

Abstract

Organizations have the task of performing and achieving results. In this context, IT organizations should be kept simple and functional so that they can provide excellent services for the business departments and the company's customers.

In this context, process organization answers the questions of "WHAT is to be done?" and "WHO does WHAT?"

3.1 The Four Ways of Integrating IT into the Business Organization

We will start with the classic assignment functions known from business administration, which first clarify how the IT organization is integrated in the company. In general, these are the following four organizational forms, which are still very widespread in medium-sized companies today (see Fig. 3.1):

- The IT organization as a department within a division.
- The IT organization as an independent division.
- The IT organization as a staff unit.
- IT in a matrix organization as centralized and at the same time decentralized IT.

V. Johanning, *Organization and Management of IT*,
https://doi.org/10.1007/978-3-658-39572-8_3

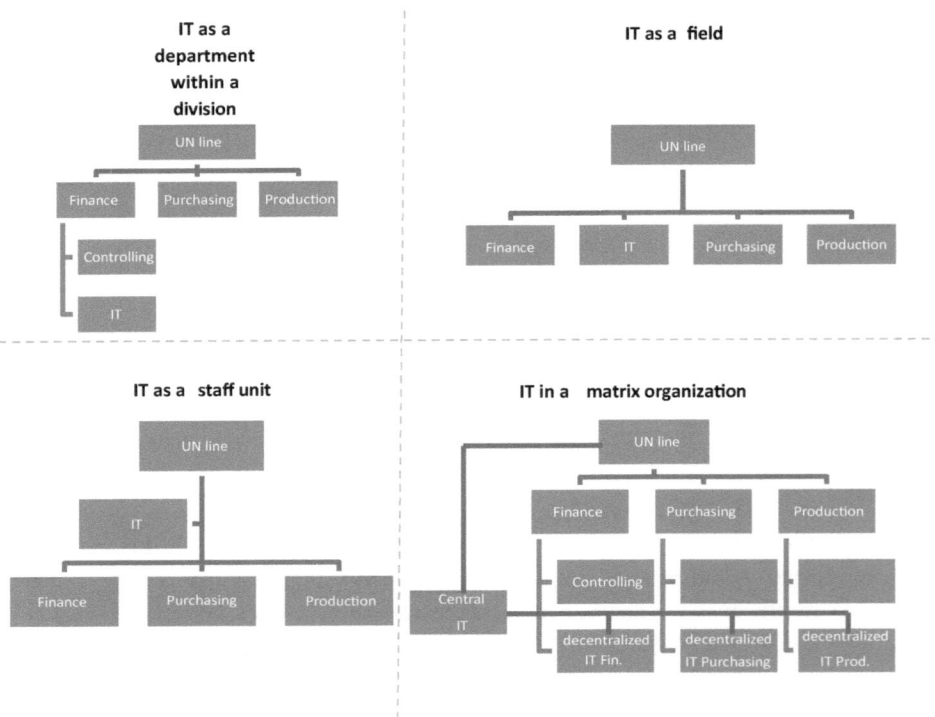

Fig. 3.1 Overview of the four classic IT organizational forms

3.1.1   Advantages and Disadvantages

In order to describe the four typical forms of organization in more detail and examine the management structure and at the same time their advantages and disadvantages in more detail, Table 3.1 serves.

Table 3.1 makes it clear that all of the organizational forms mentioned have not only advantages but also significant disadvantages. Therefore, very specific forms of organization have often emerged for IT in the past, which will be presented and examined in more detail in the following.

Overall, it should be noted that the field of IT organization design has not yet been considered in great detail in the literature or in scientific papers. However, the business organizational forms as they are lived in practice today repeatedly reach their limits when applied to IT organizations. Whether this is due to the complexity of IT, to the clearly required service orientation, or to communication problems between technicians and the "others" remains to be seen. Nevertheless, it seems important here to look at other options that have now become established in practice.

Table 3.1 Advantages and disadvantages of IT organizational forms

Organizational form	Description	Advantages	Disadvantages
IT organization as a department within a division	In this case, the IT organization is not directly assigned to the company management but belongs to a department such as finance or production	Due to the divisional management (here finance), it may be that a clear focus on specific IT tasks of this division is important for the company. This would provide a clear centralization and management by the division	In such cases, IT is often strongly dominated by the associated area (in the example of finance); this often leads to other specialist areas being neglected ($\rightarrow$ lack of overall view)
			IT is – especially when belonging to the finance department – often strongly budget-oriented (the objective is concentrated on cost savings) and not according to objectives for the entire company and for all departments
IT organization as an independent division	In this case, the IT organization is directly subordinate to the company management and not to a specific area, such as finance or production	Greater customer or departmental orientation, greater flexibility and speed in decision-making, more autonomy, and more personal responsibility	Increased number of interfaces to other areas, resulting in more complexity and risk of fragmentation
			There is a latent tendency to area egoism because it takes itself too seriously

(continued)

Table 3.1 (continued)

Organizational form	Description	Advantages	Disadvantages
IT organization as a staff unit	In this type of organization, the IT organization is assigned to the company management as a direct staff unit. Staff units are formed to provide expert knowledge and to act in an advisory capacity. Important are their independence and the fact that they have no authority to issue directives, i.e., they are only active in an advisory capacity. Accordingly, they are only active in an executive capacity as a kind of IT service unit and are not allowed to make decisions themselves	IT has set clear standards and has to implement them in the interest of the company as a whole Clear focus on expertise and advisory function without authority to issue directives (no conflicts and wrangling over competencies with specialist departments)	High potential for conflict with divisions, since informal decisions are often made through consulting and expertise, as well as proximity to management, which would actually be the responsibility of the divisions
IT organization as a matrix (centralized and decentralized)	This form of organizational design combines the centralized and decentralized functions of IT in companies. There is a central IT organization that reports directly to the company management and sets the framework guidelines as well as the decentralized IT units that are assigned to the divisions. These are largely autonomous and only subordinate to the framework guidelines and standards of the central IT but can decide and act for their area in individual cases	Closer to the problems or wishes of the areas and therefore better regarded (good business IT alignment possible) Promote close cooperation with the departments	Very complex due to high level of coordination Decisions are often made slowly or half-heartedly, as central and decentralized authorities often contradict each other Often associated with high costs if central authority does not set clear standards

3.2 Overview of IT Organizational Structures

An IT organization in a company can be designed in many different ways: from an almost completely outsourced IT to an external service provider, to the model of a subsidiary, to an internal IT department.

In the following, almost all possibilities of setting up an IT organization with their goals as well as advantages and disadvantages are presented. Important in this context are two questions:

- How is the IT organization integrated into the company?
- What is the organizational structure of the IT organization "inside"?

The following principles are always important: "Structure follows strategy" and "Technology follows structure." This means that first the strategy of the company must be established; then the structure, i.e., the organization, must be created; and then the technology, i.e., the IT systems, must be designed to fit the organization.

3.2.1 The Model of the Classical IT Organization

3.2.1.1 Definition and Objectives of the Model

Even today, many medium-sized companies still have the classic IT organization with mostly two departments or teams:

- A more software-based department: often called "IT Software/ERP".
- A more hardware-oriented department: usually called "IT operations and infrastructure".

Often there is also another department that focuses on the control and coordination of the two software and hardware departments. In the past, it was called "organization" and included process management, organizational structure, and the supervision of other services. Today, it often includes project management, IT controlling, or IT governance or architecture. Sometimes it is also referred to as the "CIO office," as it coordinates and controls the sovereign tasks of IT.

An example of a classic IT department can be seen in Fig. 3.2.

3.2.1.2 Advantages and Disadvantages

A historically grown advantage of this classic organization is the separation of software and hardware to ensure management and coordination of these two different worlds. This also ensures the smooth operation of IT by a separate department, often called "IT operations and infrastructure." In times when more than 90% of operations were still done

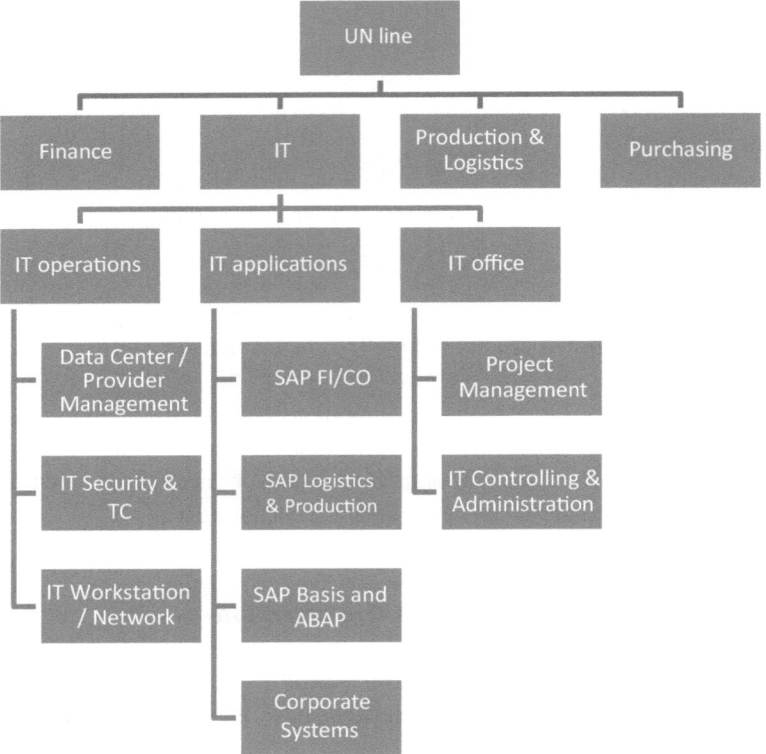

Fig. 3.2 The classic representation of an internal IT organization

internally in the company's own data center, these were the essential criteria for the company in terms of IT. Stability and security had to be guaranteed.

Through cloud computing, these values and goals are still essential but are often outsourced. One speaks of "IT from the socket" or IT as a commodity.

This brings new goals for IT into the company's focus. In the digital context, new apps should be developed as quickly as possible, solutions for Industry 4.0 must be found, and Big Data for evaluating new business opportunities are on the agenda.

This calls for a reoriented IT that must work agilely and always close to the customer instead of simply getting by with the two areas of software and operations. This means that this classic model has finally outlived its usefulness and is being replaced by new approaches, which are presented in detail in Sects. 3.2.6.1 and 3.3.5.

3.2.2 The "Plan-Build-Run" Model

3.2.2.1 Definition and Objectives of the Model

In the early 2000s, and to some extent even before, a completely new and different structuring of IT emerged, which was no longer based on the typical organizational forms from business administration outlined above. Within the framework of the so-called Plan-Build-Run concept, this internal IT is broken down into three areas:

- *Plan*: planning, management, and control (especially requirements management, IT controlling, IT architecture, IT project office, IT processes).
- *Build*: creation, further development, and maintenance of application(s) (application development or customizing of all application(s) as well as test and quality management).
- *Run*: support and maintenance of the IT infrastructure and IT operations as well as the IT hotline.

After the model became established at the end of the last millennium, it enjoyed increasing popularity in the following years and can still be found in some IT organizations today. It has evolved over time and has been absorbed into other organizational forms, e.g., the so-called Source-Make-Deliver concept by Brenner/Zarnekow [1], which was developed at the University of St. Gallen around 2003. This concept has already located IT much more strongly within the framework of a market mechanism and is accordingly a successful further development (Fig. 3.3).

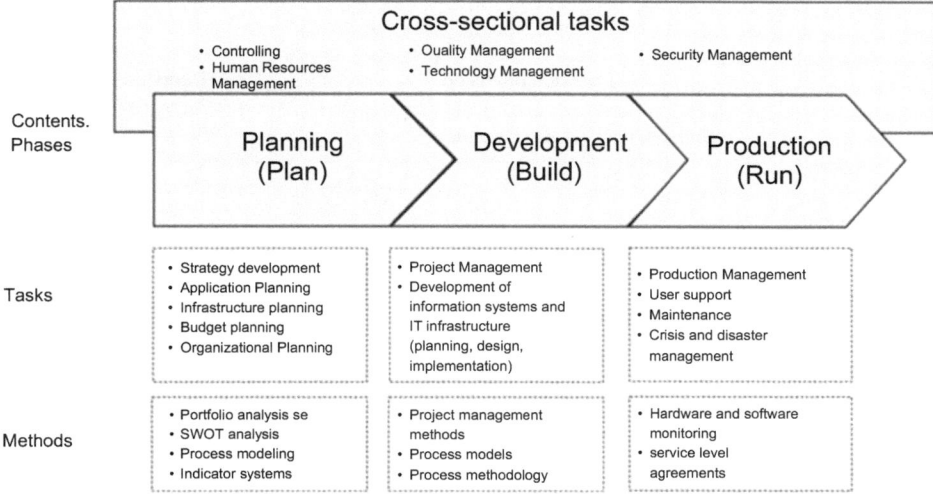

Fig. 3.3 The plan-build-run model

3.2.2.2 Advantages and Disadvantages

A significant advantage of Plan-Build-Run is the strong internal view of IT, which focuses in great detail on the key performance aspects of IT, namely, stability, availability, data security, and IT security. This is very well ensured by this model.

However, this strongly inward-looking view of IT can also be seen as a glaring disadvantage in today's prevailing dynamics of digital transformation. This is because the interfaces to the specialist departments are laid out in the plan, but are not universal in all IT processes. The problem becomes even bigger when you look at today's software development cycles. What has just been conceptualized in the "Plan" is in many cases already outdated when it arrives in the "Build." Agility is missing, and sprints like in SCRUM are not foreseen.

The beautifully structured model is getting on in years and unfortunately no longer sustainable in this fast-paced world.

3.2.3   The Source-Make-Deliver Model

3.2.3.1 Definition and Objectives of the Model

The further development of "Plan-Build-Run," significantly designed by Brenner and Zarnekow at ISG in St. Gallen [2], is based on the established process model for supply chain management: the so-called SCOR model (SCOR, supply chain operations reference).

The SCOR model divides the management processes of a company into five process areas: Plan, Source, Make, Deliver, and Return. These were used by Brenner and Zarnekow for mapping to IT concerns, as can be seen in Fig. 3.4.

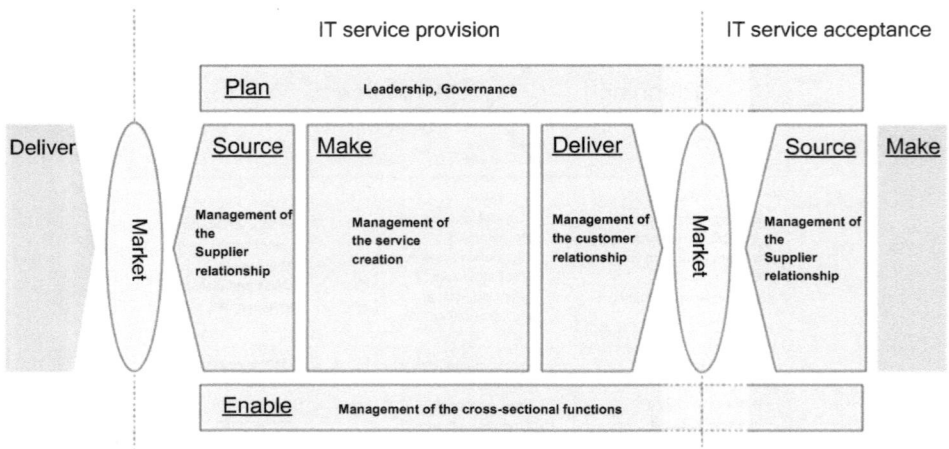

Fig. 3.4 The Source-Make-Deliver model

Following the Plan-Build-Run model, a differentiation is also made here between IT service provision and IT service acceptance. This is how the three essential core processes of an IT organization are created:

- *Source*: Source refers to the procurement process. This includes supplier management and the procurement of all resources required for IT. This includes, for example, software and hardware but also IT services, such as for software development or the operation of the IT infrastructure.
- *Make*: This refers to the provision of services within IT. This includes development, portfolio management, and production management.
- *Deliver*: This refers to the provision of IT services. This includes the management of the customer relationship, the recording of customer requirements, and the operational control of the customer interface.

Another process described is the "PLAN" process, which includes leadership and governance tasks.

3.2.3.2 Advantages and Disadvantages

More emphasis is placed on customer proximity and satisfying customer needs than in the Plan-Build-Run paradigm.

The following advantages result (according to Zarnekow and Brenner [2]):

- Tasks and roles of IT service provision and IT service acceptance are clearly separated.
- A customer-supplier relationship exists between the IT service provider and the IT service purchaser, which is handled via an internal or external market.
- For the first time, products form the basis of the exchange of services.

The disadvantages for this model of mapping an IT organization can be the often too complex seeming mapping of this model in practice. Business departments and also IT management often find it difficult to implement such a model and, above all, to really live with best practices in everyday life.

3.2.4 The Innovate-Design-Transform Model

3.2.4.1 Definition and Objectives of the Model

The current evolution of Plan-Build-Run over Source-Make-Deliver leads to a model developed by Ahlemann and Urbach called "Innovate-Design-Transform" [3].

In order to be able to meet the challenges in IT management outlined above, it requires a new target image of the IT organization in which the requirements for the ability to innovate, design, and transform can be met. The new paradigm Innovate-Design-Transform

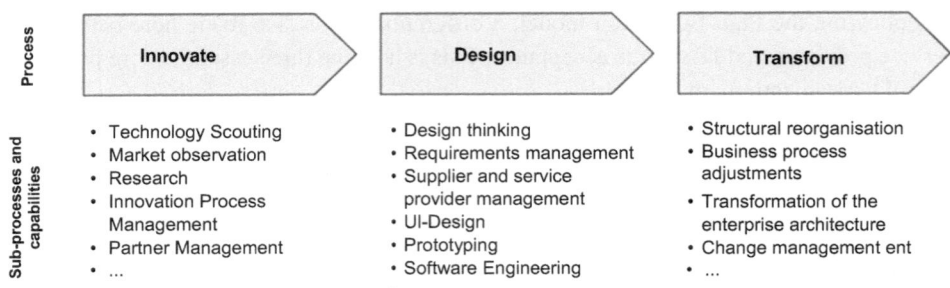

Fig. 3.5 The innovate-design-transform model

(IDT model) makes it possible to meet the three core points of the requirements for a new paradigm (Fig. 3.5).

According to Ahlemann and Urbach, the three core elements of the new model are defined as follows [3]:

- *Innovate*: The aim here is to develop new and innovative business and value creation models together with the specialist departments and external partners. This approach is characterized by creativity, agility, and flexibility. Central question: With which IT-supported innovation business and value creation models can the company become more successful?
- *Design*: The previously developed innovation ideas are translated here into detailed concepts for innovative and customer-oriented solutions and IT/IS services. The focus is on functional designs and ergonomics, but also on efficiency and effectiveness of the solutions. Central question: What should solutions and IT/IS services for implementing the innovations look like?
- *Transform*: After the innovation has been transferred into designs (and implemented), it is now a matter of changing the company in such a way that the new business or value creation model is executed. This primarily involves structural, process, and cultural changes, which require intensive change management. Central question: How is the overall organization to be changed so that the innovations are actually applied and make the company more successful?

3.2.4.2 Advantages and Disadvantages

According to Ahlemann and Urbach [3], the following are the essential paradigms of modern IT organizations, from which the new model of "Innovate-Design-Transform" is derived:

1. Innovativeness.
2. Design capacity.

3. Transformation capability.

A significant advantage over other or older models such as Plan-Build-Run lies in the joint design of new IT products with the business units, which can lead to real innovations along the entire value chain of the company due to the close integration between IT and business units.

The focus of this model is less on the previously so important implementation or programming competence but more today on essential topics such as creativity, flexibility, design competence, and also partner management. This also goes hand in hand with a cultural change. While many IT organizations have tried to establish a service culture for many years, it is now much more about a culture of innovation that also includes entrepreneurial and risk-oriented actions and decisions.

3.2.5   Shared Service Models

3.2.5.1 Definition and Objectives of the Model
In the mid-2000s, the aforementioned service function of IT often led to IT organizations being spun off into the so-called shared service centers. Separate companies were created that offered IT as a service to the company and in some cases also provided IT services to external third parties.

In some cases, the IT organizations were not directly outsourced to their own companies, but were transformed into units that functioned as internal shared service centers in the form of internal outsourcing. The important thing here was that a kind of customer relationship was created with the IT shared service center vis-à-vis the company's specialist departments.

3.2.5.2 Advantages and Disadvantages
It was hoped that this would have the following advantages:

- Greater transparency with regard to IT costs: Prices for IT services had to be established for the first time.
- Due to the emerging market mechanism, IT should be more aware of supply and demand for IT services, instead of just reacting to requests from the business department.
- IT management should act in an entrepreneurial way and not simply – as before – administer.
- A stronger customer orientation and thus a better service quality should be achieved.
- IT services should be standardized as best as possible.
- Benchmarking of IT performance should be possible for the management to make transparent for the first time how good or bad IT actually is.

Shared service concepts can still be found today. They had a very great influence on the further development of IT in the direction of service mentality, transparency, and customer orientation, which today has merged into the demand-supply concept. This concept, with its current status as of 2014, is to serve as the basis for this book. The working questions are also based on this. Before taking a closer look at the demand-supply concept, however, the current IT organization of the example company should be examined. It shows very vividly the path from the typical IT organization found in more than 90% of companies in the 2000s to the demand-supply concept.

3.2.6   The Demand-Supply Model

Based on the "Plan-Build-Run," the IT organizations of medium-sized and larger companies as well as corporate groups have often gone the way of subdividing the IT organization into two large subdivisions instead of three:

- The demand organization (called Demand).
- The supply organization (called supply).

Therefore, one speaks of the so-called demand-supply organization, as it is exemplified in Fig. 3.6.

Through the demand-supply organization model, IT can grow out of the technology role and, with the demand branch (formerly PLAN and/or specialist department), move much closer to the specialist departments and the company management in order to recognize and satisfy the requirements there early and proactively in the form of demand. The top management is also actively involved and specifies the strategy on the basis of which IT can map the procurement and demand structures in the company as a kind of market. The service branch (formerly BUILD and RUN) is the former technical core of IT, which as Supply provides the IT services according to the demand from Demand.

In concrete terms, this means for the design of the IT organization that the demand branch mainly contains the following areas or departments:

- Request and change management (requirements management).
- Cost/benefit and profitability analyses.
- Process management (depending on the case, this is either more in the specialist area or in demand IT)

The supply branch can be operated both internally and externally, but also as a kind of hybrid of internal and external components. Supply includes the provision of IT services in the form of applications and their basis through infrastructure/operation. The following areas or departments are typical in the supply branch:

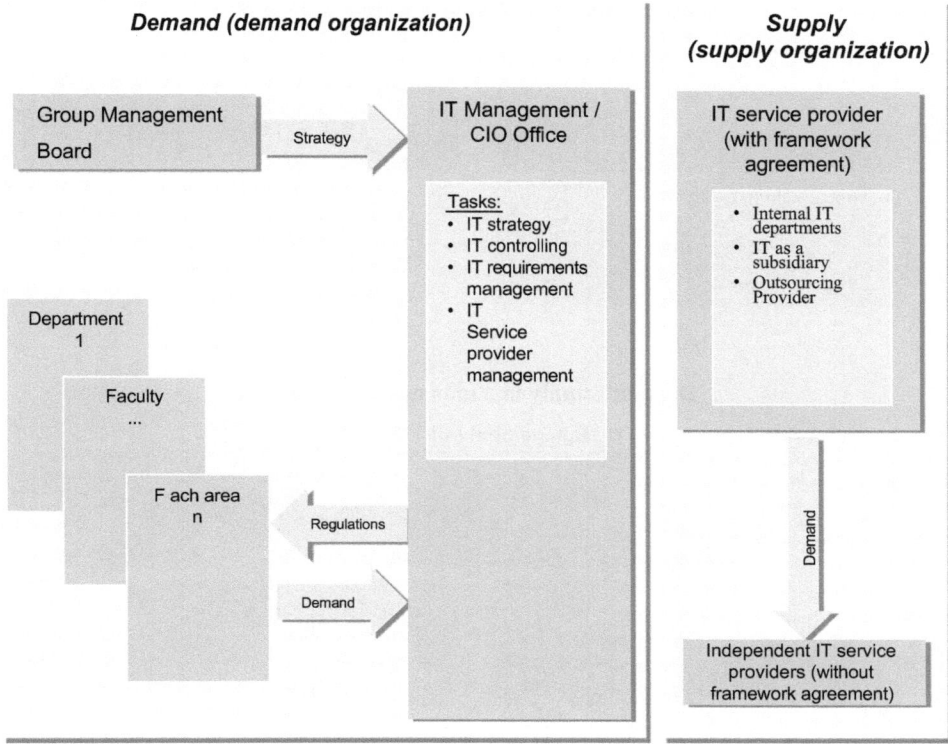

Fig. 3.6 IT demand and supply organization at a glance. (According to Gadatsch [4])

- Application development and support.
- IT quality and test management.
- Operations and infrastructure.

The key question now is: Who will lead the Demand branch and who will lead the Supply branch, or will both be managed centrally? What happens with the "cross-sectional tasks" such as strategy, project management, or architecture: Do these belong to Demand or Supply? Three different models are possible here, which are also shown as a blueprint in Fig. 3.7:

- Decentralized demand IT: Has a CIO office for the Demand branch and a CTO office for the Supply branch (note: CIO stands for chief information officer and CTO stands for chief technology officer).

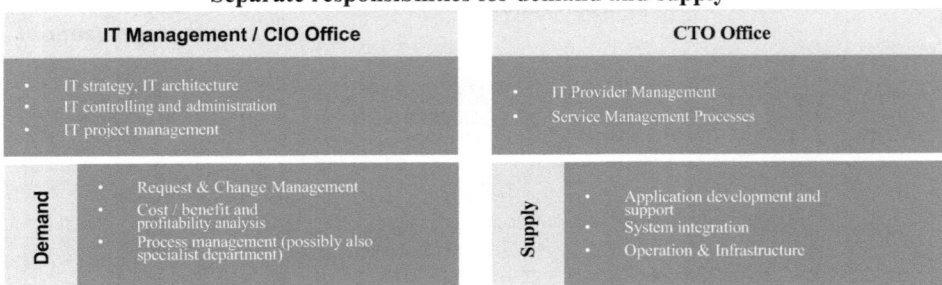

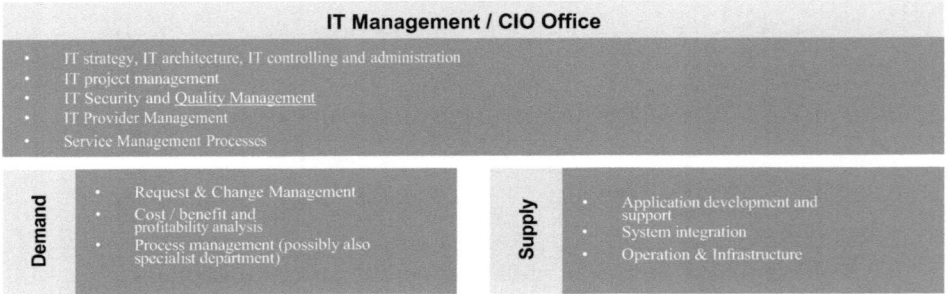

Fig. 3.7 Blueprint for Demand-Supply organization

- Centralized demand IT: The same as decentralized demand IT, except that the demand managers are directly responsible for requirements and process management instead of the CIO office.
- Demand/Supply in one CIO office: Both branches have a common CIO office.

Generally, the following departments or divisions are located in the CIO office of the Demand branch:

- IT strategy, IT architecture (whereby the question of sovereignty over the IT architecture is quite contentious and many companies also see the IT architecture in the supply branch)
- IT controlling and administration
- IT project management

The Supply branch of the CTO office includes the following departments or divisions that provide services across Supply:

- IT provider management
- Service management processes (definition and standards for the competence centers of the supply branch)

If there is only one CIO office for Demand and Supply, the abovementioned areas are managed together in this office.

The areas of "IT security" and "IT quality and test management" are also often found as cross-sectional functions in the supply branch. However, many companies have also integrated these as a separate competence center in the supply branch or, due to the importance for the company, at least the area of "IT security" in the CIO office.

With this division into demand and supply, IT establishes itself as a two-part organization that is much more closely integrated into the business and the specialist department with the demand part and can therefore design, control, and moderate more proactively. The supply part is the real "factory" in which IT services are developed, customized, operated, and supported. With clearly defined interfaces between demand and supply, this can be done either by an internal organization or by external partners or a mixture of both.

3.2.6.1 Advantages and Disadvantages of the Demand/Supply Model

The advantages of the demand/supply concept can be illustrated as follows:

- Business IT alignment: IT services can be clearly and comprehensibly derived from the business requirements. A business case can be calculated for services.
- Separation of IT demand and IT supply: By separating demand and supply, the conflict of interest between the best possible individual IT solution and cost-reducing standardization can be resolved.
- Transparency is created with regard to costs, services, and tasks.
- Shorter decision-making processes and clear responsibilities lead to an improvement in efficiency.
- Clearer task and role definitions as well as better demarcation from the tasks of the specialist departments ensure employee motivation.

A disadvantage that is often presented is that the supply part is too far removed from the business. In general, however, it should be noted that when coupled with modern methods of agile software development, e.g., in the form of SCRUM, the demand-supply model is certainly future-proof and represents a well-suited model for the design of an IT organization.

3.3   Special Features of the Organizational Structure of IT

3.3.1   DevOps

DevOps is a made-up word consisting of "development" and "operations" (IT operations). Through a much closer cooperation of these two areas, a greatly improved IT performance in the form of higher speed in development, more efficient delivery, and better quality of the software is to be achieved.

The understanding of roles – often shaped by the Plan-Build-Run model often used in practice (see Sect. 3.2.1.2) – led to silo thinking between development and IT operations. Often, a finished software development was simply thrown over the fence from the Build to the Run, where no one knew anything about it. This led to delays in the delivery of the software and the quality also suffered.

Through DevOps, methods and processes have been developed that make this collaboration much more effective. Often, the respective protagonists from Build and Run sit together in one room in order to be constantly informed about the current status and thus already design everything in the development phase in such a way that it fits for the operational phase.

Figure 3.8 schematically shows the flow of a DevOps model.

The "Plan-Code-Build-Test" processes take place in the Dev part. The "Release" process takes place jointly between Dev and Ops, and on the Ops side, responsibility is then assumed for the "Deploy-Operate-Monitor" processes. The dovetailing of code development and code execution is also referred to as "continuous integration." Specific continuous integration software has been available for several years to ensure that code quality is improved.

Also in the context of DevOps is the notion of continuous delivery. This is a software development method where code changes are automatically created, tested, and prepared for a production release. Continuous delivery is an extension of continuous integration. In it, all code changes are deployed to a test and/or production environment after they have been designed. With a proper implementation of continuous delivery, developers always have a creation artifact available for deployment that has already gone through a standardized testing process.

Fig. 3.8 Schematic representation of the DevOps model

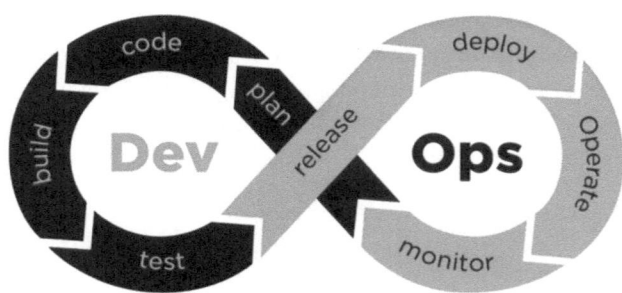

3.3.2   BizOps or BizDevOps

When it comes to better integration between IT and business, there has been a lot of talk about professional requirements management or agile teams or product management. This is all not wrong, but there is now a new approach that finally brings together the business drivers and the concerns of IT, always focusing on the benefits and added value of each IT project. It is called "BizOps!"

BizOps is basically an extension of DevOps. DevOps, for example, aims to deliberately break down the two silos of software development and IT operations and closely interlink them. BizOps now takes this idea to the next level, because it is no longer about agile IT alone, but about better and faster results in the company as a whole. Through BizOps, decisions are not only accelerated, but are always subject to at least one benefit criterion for the company.

An important factor here is that the specialist department, as the customer, is involved in processes at an early stage and cooperation between teams is improved.

What does this look like in practice?

BizOps teams consist of IT and business staff and can be used for different tasks:

1. Closely tied to a department for specific but mission-critical tasks
2. Directly linked to the management for strategic planning and development as well as validation of new IT-, data-, or technology-driven business models
3. Involved in IT, but with a strong connection to a specialist area or process topic (ideally disciplinary in IT with specialist leadership from the specialist area as well as a job in both IT and the specialist area)

What does such a BizOps team need?

The typical skillset of a BizOps employee might look like this:

- Change attitude
- Implementer and doer qualities
- Empathy
- Agile and flexible mindset
- Generalist rather than specialist – all-rounder
- IT background
- Strategic knowledge and business model know-how

An ideal extension of the BizOps idea is the combination with DevOps to form a concept that could be called BizDevOps. This gives the actual end-to-end responsibility for an IT product from the business department to development to operations.

If one wanted to represent this extension of BizDevOps graphically, it would look like Fig. 3.9.

blueprint

Fig. 3.9 Overview of BizDevOps

3.3.3   A Bimodal IT Organization

One speaks of a bimodal IT when the IT organization is split into two parts. One part can be called the "traditional IT," with a conventional development and operations organization. The second part is the "new" or better "agile IT," which leads projects on a kind of fast track to the goal with high speed and innovation requirements as well as the methods necessary for this. Figure 3.10 shows the bimodal IT organization in a matrix with the axes "speed" and "stability/reliability." It can be clearly seen that "agile IT" achieves results much faster than "traditional IT"; the latter, however, has the advantage of somewhat greater stability and reliability. Depending on what is required in the company, a choice can be made between these two types of IT organization. App development as a digital service to a product should be quickly available in the market and therefore needs more the agile approach of "agile IT." ERP projects can be successful in a mixture of both approaches.

Bimodal IT has emerged as a result of higher demands in the digital context, because the product cycles have not only rapidly decreased in automotive engineering or smartphones. In software development, too, the life cycle of an app developed today is already outdated in a few months. Table 3.2 illustrates the differences between traditional and agile IT and thus gets to the heart of why many CIOs want bimodal IT.

Because the complete change of IT to only modern development methods is often not so easy. Bulky legacy systems, the huge ERP, and other old treasures often prevent the complete change. A way out is then a bimodal IT in order to be able to deliver at least for demanding customers.

However, bimodal IT is seen by many experts only as a kind of transitional model toward a fully agile IT organization. Furthermore, the bimodal approach fails in many cases due to an absolutely understandable, human characteristic: No one wants to be one of the "slow ones." For example, at the end of 2017, the CIO of BMW refrained from the

Fig. 3.10 The bimodal IT
organization

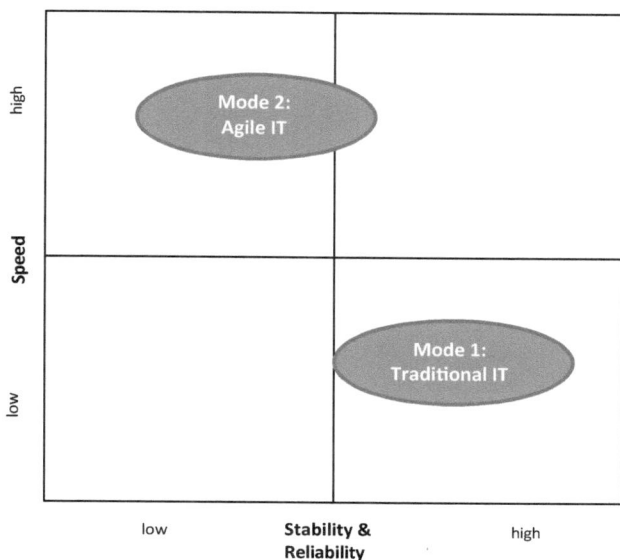

Table 3.2 The difference between traditional and agile IT

	Traditional IT	Agile IT
Destination	Stability and reliability	Innovation and differentiation
Focus	System-centric	User-centric
Planning horizon	Long term	Short term
Methods	Plan-driven	Iterative and agile
Development cycles	Long	Briefly
Development and operation	Strictly separated	Integrated

Source: Volker Johanning

bimodal model or "two-speed IT" for exactly this reason, in order to convert all projects to
"100 percent agile" [5]. This shows very clearly that "mixed approaches" are mostly well-
intentioned, but cannot be implemented at all in practice. More on the methods necessary
to introduce 100% agile are presented in Sect. 3.3.5.

3.3.4   The IT Organization in an International Context

Germany has been the export world champion for many years. Most companies are therefore globally positioned with many production facilities and sales offices around the world.

What does this mean for the IT organization? How can IT organize itself to meet this
global demand for high standards in terms of IT as well?

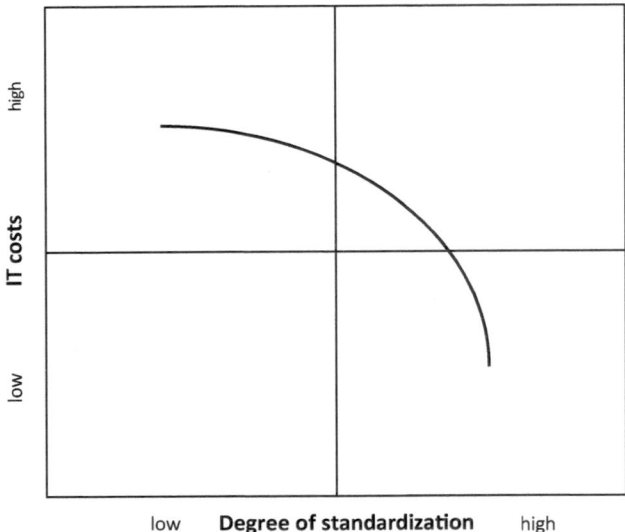

Fig. 3.11   IT in an international context

From the perspective of IT and the CIO, the focus is on standardization – both at the level of IT system standards and in terms of IT costs in a global context.

As can be seen in Fig. 3.11, IT costs decrease with the degree of standardization. This is the main reason why IT systems should be as close to standard as possible for internationally operating companies all over the world. The same applies to process efficiency: The greater the degree of standardization of the IT system, the greater the process efficiency of the company.

For the structure of the IT organization, this means that the IT standards must be enforced worldwide and therefore a central IT organization must be responsible for the specifications of these IT standards.

In general, there are two ways of structuring IT in an international context:

1. Headquarter-oriented IT organization = central IT management.
2. Plant-oriented IT organization = decentralized IT management.

In the first case of the headquarter-oriented IT organization, IT decisions can be or are made centrally at headquarters. This means that IT standards can be enforced in all plants and branches, which leads to the cost/process efficiencies shown.

On the other hand, decentralized IT management is also possible, in which the plants or subsidiaries set up and manage their own system landscape. This can make sense for very different products and processes. If, for example, a plant in the USA manufactures completely different products than the plant in China and the processes are also completely different, then a decentralized IT organization makes perfect sense.

A compromise between centralized and decentralized is also possible. In this case, for example, only certain processes are specified from headquarters, and others can be adapted individually and decentrally to the respective needs.

Furthermore, in addition to the IT system landscape, the operation, infrastructure, and, above all, support must also be considered. Here, centralized and decentralized approaches can also be considered, whereby support will only function globally to a limited extent. Instead, this must rather take place locally, at least for issues that can only be fulfilled physically on-site.

From the user's point of view, international IT should meet the following requirements in terms of globally standardized IT:

- The same operating system and user accounts: the same login procedures (accounts) everywhere for all branches of the company.
- The same hardware: support and maintenance are the same everywhere, and you can help each other.
- A user can log on to the company network anywhere in the world with the same user account and password.
- The same office and e-mail software is used everywhere for better communication between all employees worldwide.
- With regard to ERP, the same rules exist worldwide – at least for the master data.
- Financial reports are structured in the same way everywhere and are therefore comparable.
- CRM commonalities: worldwide customer database, so that customers who are also globally active do not appear in x databases, but only once in a CRM database (this generates synergies in the customer approach).
- The same collaboration tools are used for easy exchange among each other.
- The service desk is the same or standardized everywhere.

3.3.5   Line-Centric Versus Project-Centric IT Organization

IT organizations are always also project organizations. Since in most cases the project organization leads an existence in the shadow of the actual IT organization with the disciplinary responsibilities, there is an increased conflict of competencies due to unclear responsibilities.

The differentiation between professional and disciplinary responsibility is only one issue. Another issue in this context is the "loan" of employees from the disciplinary line organization to a temporary project organization. Here, problems often arise not only between the project manager and the disciplinary superior, but the project employees also suffer from unresolved conflicts at another level.

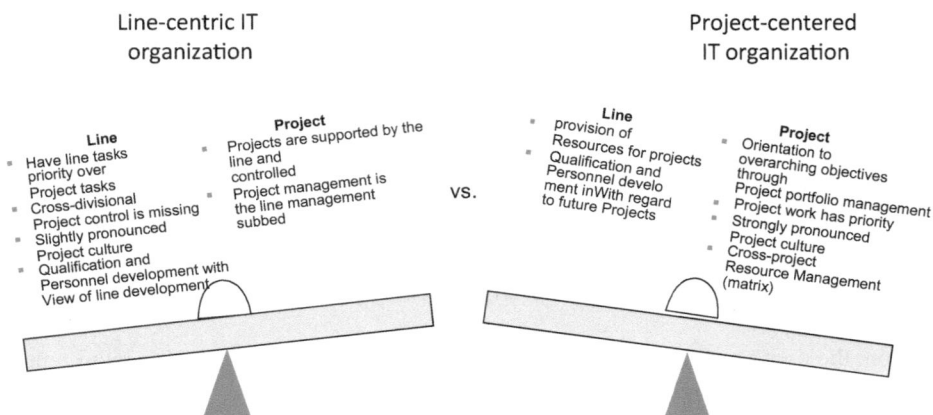

Fig. 3.12 Line-centric versus project-centric IT organization

This outlined everyday problem corresponds to the most frequently occurring so-called line-centric IT organization. In contrast, there is the project-centered IT organization, which is contrasted with the line-centered organization in Fig. 3.12.

The line-centric IT organization is characterized by a clearly structured, often functional organizational form. Due to this characteristic, the line managers have more power than the project managers and see their daily business as having priority over the temporary projects. Projects are largely organized across lines. Due to the rule of the line, however, project coordination across line boundaries is always very difficult for the project manager. Under these circumstances, a distinctive project culture cannot develop, since each employee tends to orient himself to his line organization in order to be able to make a long-term career. In such cases, the topic of personnel development and qualification is also more strongly influenced by the line. There is not so much focus on temporary project skills, but more on the line organization's own specialization. Responsibility for projects lies with line managers who commission and supervise projects. Accordingly, the project manager is always subordinate to a line manager.

The project-centric IT organization, on the other hand, is characterized by the fact that the focus is not on the line with day-to-day business but on advancing IT projects. To this end, there is cross-line coordination in the form of project management offices that are directly attached to the CIO. This is where the prioritization, evaluation, and commissioning of IT projects take place with the support of project portfolios. Business-IT alignment takes center stage in such organizational forms and is pushed through projects with the business units. The line organizations provide the personnel for the projects and coordinate and ensure the balance between line tasks (day-to-day business) and project tasks. Qualification and personnel development is strongly oriented toward large project(s) and is derived from the needs and requirements of the specialist departments. For large projects, it is important that the project or program manager is independent of line decisions, which is why he or she often reports directly to the CIO in a kind of project pool.

3.4   Agile Methods in IT Organization Design

Trailer
The digital transformation and the start-up world have contributed to the fact that IT organizations are also undergoing a major change. In particular, agile methods, the systemic approach, and network structures are the efficiency drivers of a modern IT organization.

3.4.1   SCRUM

3.4.1.1 Definition and Objectives of SCRUM
SCRUM is not a form of organization, but a project management method that uses the agile mindset, especially in software development.

The term "SCRUM" is not an abbreviation but comes from rugby and means something like "tight scrum." In rugby, this always occurs when all players gather around the ball. In terms of software development, the idea behind this is that the development of software by lone warriors is no longer up to today's requirements of speed and flexibility. SCRUM starts here by putting the team idea in the foreground. Instead of a dense scrum, only the back-and-forth play of the ball according to rules is supposed to create success in software development in terms of speed and flexibility.

This form of self-organization of a developer team does not need rigid project rules or an explicit project manager. A SCRUM master ensures that the rules of SCRUM are adhered to in the development process.

This SCRUM master is therefore responsible for the processes. In contrast to the product owner, who, as the person responsible for the product, defines and prioritizes the requirements on his own. Within a so-called sprint, in which the development takes place, the development team must not be disturbed and can fully concentrate on its tasks.

SCRUM is relatively simple and can be used immediately to develop in a structured yet flexible manner. SCRUM works empirically, incrementally, and iteratively, which means that the application is based on experience, in small steps and repetitive stages.

3.4.1.2 The Functioning and Artifacts of SCRUM
SCRUM consists of the so-called artifacts that describe how SCRUM works. These include the process, the roles, and the artifacts or documents themselves. These are presented below for better understanding and are shown graphically in Fig. 3.13.

Generally speaking, a SCRUM process is divided into the so-called sprints, which can last between 2 weeks and a maximum of 4 weeks.

A sprint consists of the following components:

- The "SPRINT PLANNING".
- The "DAILY SCRUMS": The Daily SCRUM lasts 15 min. Each team member briefly answers three questions:

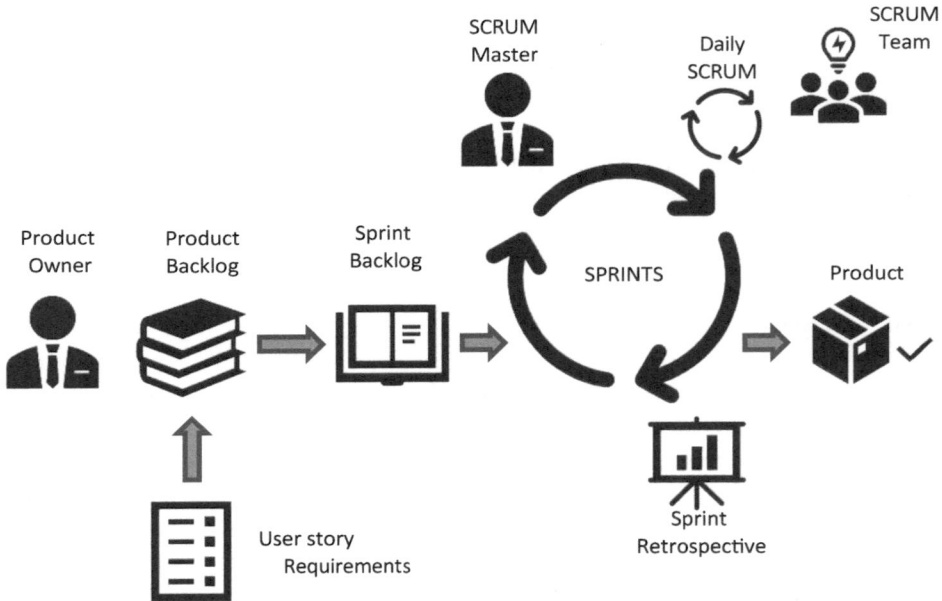

Fig. 3.13 Overview of the SCUM method

1. What have I done since the last Daily SCRUM?
2. What was holding me back?
3. What will I do until the next Daily SCRUM?
- The "SPRINT REVIEW".
- The "SPRINT RETROSPECTIVE": What have we learned? What can be improved?

As can be seen in Fig. 3.13, the SCRUM process delivers a first, functional (!) product at the end. This is presented to the client, who checks this product and gives feedback on what is still missing, should be different, or already fits. This feedback from the client is now incorporated back into the product backlog, and the SCRUM process begins anew.

The following three roles are important in the SCRUM process:

Product Owner
It represents the users of the product or the stakeholders of the project. In the case of software, for example, this would be the users who want the process to run smoothly. In the case of a product, it is the product managers who represent their customers.

Team
The team organizes itself; due to its small size (two to nine team members), it does not need a classic project manager. Therefore, it does not receive any instructions on how to

proceed. Due to its interdisciplinary structure, software architects can be found there as well as, for example, programmers, quality assurance specialists, and testers.

SCRUM Master

He assumes the function of a moderator. This means that he ensures that the theory, practices, and rules of the SCRUM method are adhered to in the team. In addition, he is the contact person for outsiders by clarifying which interactions with the team are beneficial and which are not.

In addition, as shown in Fig. 3.13, there are three artifacts or documents to perform the SCRUM process according to the rules:

Product Backlog

The product backlog is a to-do list with requirements. It is constantly developed and maintained by the product owner. Since the product backlog is dynamic, it is never complete – the product owner constantly adapts it to the product.

Sprint Backlog

From the requirements of the product backlog, a selection of requirements is made that the team will work on within a sprint. The individual tasks in the sprint backlog are called tickets. Each team member takes responsibility for their own ticket. The sprint backlog provides a forecast of the extent to which the next increment will be functional or what work is still needed to deliver a functional Done. The KANBAN board is often used here for better visualization.

Product Increment

At the end of each sprint, there is a functional intermediate product – the product increment. It must be ready for use even if the product owner does not want to deliver it yet.

What is missing now are the rules and planning for the SCRUM process. Here, four essential meetings are planned:

Sprint Planning

In Sprint Planning, the team plans the next sprint. The requirements are broken down into concrete tasks. These should be able to be processed within 1 day. Great importance is attached to efficient communication; this is practiced "face to face" and not merely by handing over documents. The result of Sprint Planning is the sprint backlog.

Daily SCRUM

At the beginning of each working day, the team meets for a maximum quarter-hour meeting, the Daily SCRUM. It is preferably held standing up, as this is intended to promote concentration on important points. Once a day, this ensures an exchange with all team members. Each team member briefly explains his or her state of affairs:

- What has been done since the last meeting?
- What is planned until the next meeting?
- What obstacles/problems are hindering progress?

Problems that cannot be solved within 15 min are handed over to the SCRUM master. Daily SCRUM is an essential means for reflection and self-organization of the team.

Sprint Review
At the end of each sprint, there is a Sprint Review. Here, the development team presents the product increment (in the sense of "Done"). The product is reviewed, and the product backlog is adjusted if necessary. The product owner as well as the stakeholders can give input, but the final decision on whether to change requirements rests with the product owner.

Sprint Retrospective
The retrospective is about reviewing the work of the project team in order to continuously improve it. Central questions here are, for example:

- What has hindered cooperation?
- What was particularly conducive to the collaboration?
- Which new approaches should be given greater consideration?

Not directly part of the official part of SCRUM but still recommendable is another meeting: the **Lesson Learned** or **Fuck-up Hour**.

The followers of agility want to deal constructively with mistakes. That is why they talk openly about setbacks and their lessons at the Fuck-up Hour. This is not only instructive but also strengthens trust in the team.

As a short conclusion, it can be said that the SCRUM method can be implemented quickly with few tools due to its very good structure and creates real transparency during implementation or when struggling with projects that do not get finished.

3.4.2   IT KANBAN

3.4.2.1 Definition and Objectives of KANBAN in IT

KANBAN originally comes from the automotive industry. It was developed by Taiichi Ohno at Toyota back in 1947 and is a core component of the so-called Toyota Production System (TPS). In the TPS, cards are used to signal to the respective upstream production area what is to be produced and in what quantities. The resulting just-in-time production only produces exactly what is really needed.

Exactly this principle can also be applied in software development. David Anderson transferred this concept to this area. He integrated the basic idea of KANBAN with fundamental principles – from both Lean Production and Lean Product Development – and supplemented them with the Theory of Constraints as well as classic risk management [6].

KANBAN is therefore – just like SCRUM – not an organizational model, but a method for job control and monitoring in IT.

3.4.2.2 How KANBAN Works in IT

David Anderson, one of the founders of agile software development, described four basic principles and six practices that companies incorporate into their way of working when applying KANBAN.

The four basic principles (the so-called foundational principles) are:

- Basic principle 1: "Start with what you do now!" – Start with what you are doing right now.
- Core principle 2: **Agree to** pursue incremental, evolutionary change.
- Principle 3: "Respect the current process, roles, responsibilities and titles" – Respect current processes, roles, responsibilities, and titles.
- Principle 4: "Encourage acts of leadership at all levels in your organization – from individual contributor to senior management" – Encourage acts of leadership at all levels of the organization – from individual contributors to senior management.

An essential aspect of these principles is the idea that, for the time being, nothing needs to be changed in the existing situation. Although KANBAN sees itself as an evolutionary form of change management, the changes arise gradually from the concrete application of the KANBAN principle.

The following six practices according to Anderson are especially effective when implementing the first steps with KANBAN:

Principle 1: Visualization of the Work
Often the individual process steps of the value chain are made visible with a whiteboard. This is designed with post-it to form a KANBAN board on which the columns represent the individual stations (see Fig. 3.14). The individual tasks, features, user stories, and the like are written on the sticky notes (optionally also index cards), which move from left to right on the KANBAN board in the course of the process.

Principle 2: Limitation and Limitation of Work
To ensure an even workflow, the number of tickets (work in progress – WiP) that can be processed at a station at the same time is limited. If a station is currently working on three tickets and this station has been limited to three tickets, it is not allowed to accept another fourth ticket, even if the station working on it could deliver another one. This procedure is called the pull principle: Each station collects its work from the predecessor station, instead of simply passing completed work to the next station. In this way, each station also has the chance to work off its tasks.

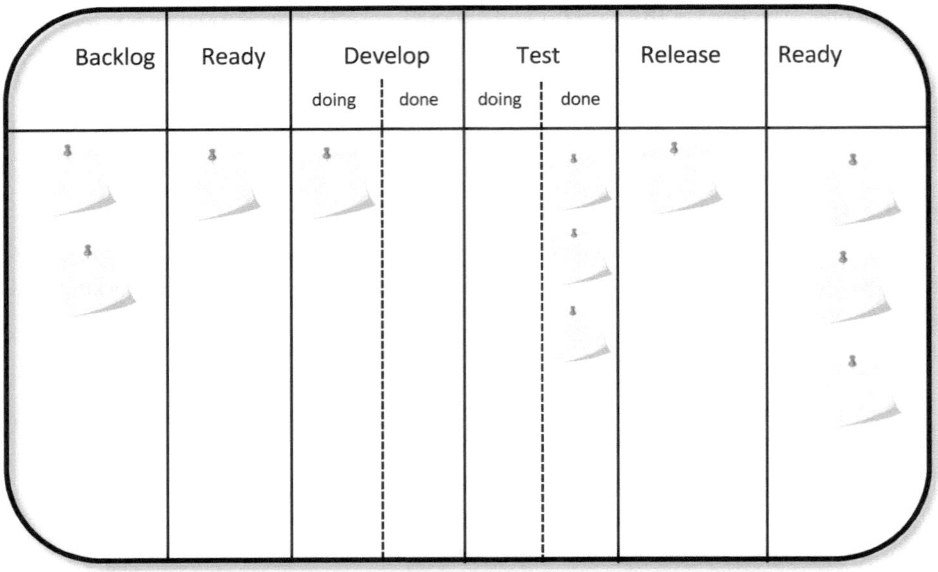

Fig. 3.14 KANBAN in IT – the board

Principle 3: Control of the Workflow
Throughout the KANBAN process, individual areas such as queues, cycle time, and throughput are checked. This makes it possible to determine where the work is well organized and where improvements may be necessary. This also increases and optimizes reliability in the workflow at the same time.

Principle 4: Clarification and Process Rules
To ensure that all parties are working from the same assumptions and regularities, all rules must be defined. These include, for example, clarification of who draws when and under what conditions is the next ticket drawn from the waiting list?

Principle 5: Feedback
KANBAN is a flexible model; therefore, constant reviews are carried out, and feedback is given. The aim of KANBAN is to see where bottlenecks occur – a feedback system is introduced for this purpose. On the basis of feedback, each station can see where it is currently stuck, where support may be needed.

Improvement
As explained in the previous point, feedback is an important part of KANBAN. The feedback mechanisms introduced lead to improvements in that, in some stations, streamlining or additions can be made – depending on the backlog or need.

For KANBAN to be used successfully, the following three tips should be considered:

- Only one project may be currently in progress.
- There are never more than six projects on hold.
- Everyday tasks have no place on the board. Put them on a normal to-do list (KANBAN is not intended for daily organization).

3.4.3   Self-Organization and Holacracy in IT

3.4.3.1 Definition and Objectives of Self-Organization

Self-organization and holacracy are mentioned here in the same breath, and in fact, the same thing is meant. In addition, there are several other terms that basically mean similar things and always have one thing in common at the core, decisions, and thus the distribution of power; no longer take place from the top-down; but are autonomized, i.e., decisions are made where they arise. Examples of organizational forms that belong to this are:

- Agile organizations
- Democratic enterprises
- Network organizations
- Holacratic organizations
- Self-organized organizations

One thing is already clear: This form of organization almost completely abolishes hierarchies. Figure 3.15 clearly shows the difference between the classical hierarchical organization and a holacratic organization based on the principles of self-organization. The parent circle in a holacratic system corresponds to all the work that needs to be done in an

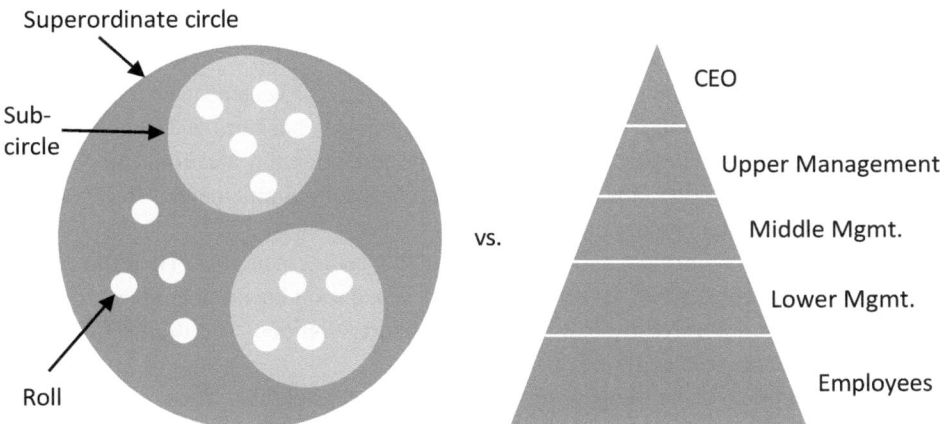

Fig. 3.15 Self-organization at a glance

organization. A sub-circle in this context is a bundle of related or similar work and the role as the smallest circle represents the person who performs the work.

The holacratic system is based on the principle of self-organization. Employees assume (personal) responsibility and organize themselves. Many IT organizations have already set out and tested some approaches to self-organization. And although decisions should always be made autonomously, it is noted everywhere: Self-organization also needs leadership and thus power.

If you look at Fig. 3.15, you might think that hierarchies no longer exist and are no longer needed. This is not true. What no longer exists is command and control. However, it must of course be clearly regulated who is responsible for what. That's why employees are organized in self-governing circles in which they can take on leadership tasks.

Anyone can contribute ideas to the circle to which she or he belongs. Functional leaders (appointed in the next higher circle) and delegates (appointed in the lower circle) act as links between the circles. There are clear responsibilities and decision-making powers in the system. A significant investment, for example, must be approved by a director of the highest circle.

Furthermore, it is important to understand that the principle of self-organization does not work without managers either. If managers remove themselves from the equation because they think the change will only affect operational and middle managers, then self-organization is doomed to fail. Rather, the model entails a redistribution of power and authority throughout the organization. In such a concept, the manager acts as a coach and designer of a framework.

On this basis, holacratic systems and self-organization for IT departments can certainly provide interesting approaches for new cooperation and, in particular, solve the difficult issue of cooperation with the business departments in the future.

3.4.4 Digital Labs

3.4.4.1 Definition and Objectives

The intention and strategy behind a digital lab is to create a protected space for generating and implementing new, innovative ideas. In the day-to-day business and ongoing operations of a company, these ideas would not receive the attention and time they need to mature and grow. In digital labs, ideas can be developed and implemented free of hierarchies, bureaucracy, and process regulations.

Digitalization does not stop at industries or existing business models. Therefore, digital labs serve as an incubator for the development of new digital business models as a transformation site from purely physical products to smart solutions. The digital future of a company is preconceived and tried out in such labs.

When it comes to terminology, you cannot stop at digital labs. These are often also called innovation labs or digital or innovation units. The goals of such a lab or unit are always very similar:

- Creation of feasibility analyses (proof of concepts, the so-called POCs), emergence of innovative ideas and products
- Joint evaluation of use cases on digital topics
- Realization of the so-called minimal viable products (MVPs), which serve to bring a product to market maturity in the fastest possible way with the maximum necessary functions
- Development and testing of digital business models
- Development of IoT and Big Data solutions
- Support in setting up own digital units (internal departments or external spin-offs)
- Creating contacts and a network with start-ups, software and digital experts, and research institutions
- Development of methodological knowledge or process models, such as design thinking, SCRUM, prototyping, or Business Model Canvas
- Training and education on digital topics

There are also very specific labs that focus on niche topics of digitalization, for example, the data labs or data analytic labs with a focus on Big Data. Then there are IoT labs, AI labs, etc. What these always have in common is their niche focus.

In addition to digital labs, there are three other forms of digital initiatives that can be very lucrative for traditional companies (see Fig. 3.16):

- The headquarters or parent company as "company builder"
- The role of the headquarters as an "incubator"
- The use of the "accelerator" construct

Figure 3.16 shows the definition and mission of these three digital initiatives, and, most importantly, it creates a distinction between them and the digital lab.

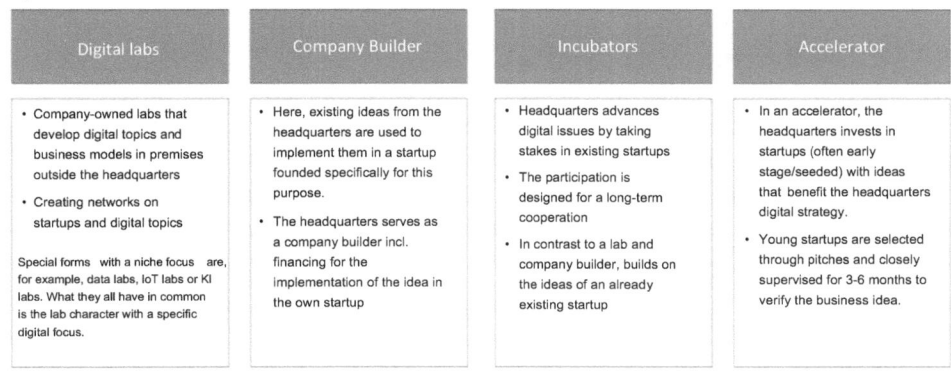

Fig. 3.16 Different forms of labs and their delimitation

In general, it can be said that with digital labs and the company builder, **new ideas** are always generated and either a separate digital lab is set up or a separate start-up is founded for this purpose (company builder). In contrast to the self-founded start-ups, the digital lab is usually located somewhat closer to the parent company. However, the biggest difference is probably that the digital lab can take on a large, colorful bouquet of digital topics and projects, while the start-up as a company has a clear, own corporate strategy and has to appear and act independently on the market (*a* clear mission). The digital lab, on the other hand, is more "attached" to the parent company and creates the shell and experimental space away from the hustle and bustle of the parent company to develop digital projects and products. So if you want to not only try out a completely new business model but bring it to market and are convinced of its maturity and customer potential, then having your own start-up makes sense, and the parent company logically acts as a company builder. If this new business model is to be tested, tried out, and matured first, then a digital lab makes more sense.

In contrast, the incubator and accelerator models focus on **existing ideas**. In the role of incubator, the parent company invests in existing start-ups and develops them further. These investments in start-ups are usually well thought out and fit very well into the parent company's digital growth strategy. When a higher-risk investment is made in an idea by founders, this is called the accelerator role. This is early stage investment (seed capital) where the parent company virtually participates in the further development of the start-up idea. It helps in the start-up formation and gives the founders a network and everything for the flourishing and especially the verification of the idea. This involvement is more short term in nature (3–6 months maximum), whereas the incubator role is more long term (6–24 months).

In the role of the accelerator, it is important to note that the parent company at least already has experience in the digital environment or can now call former start-up managers its own in its own management circles. This is because the founders need not only capital in the early phase but above all support to mature and verify and – in the case of positive market feedback – also support in scaling the idea into a product and a competitive start-up.

3.4.4.2 The Structure of a Digital Lab

Whether it is a data lab, innovation or IoT lab, or the use of artificial intelligence (AI), a digital lab is a very valuable institution to massively strengthen the competitive strength of their company in the digital age.

This strategy paper has shown how you can learn from the mistakes of previous labs. And based on these learning experiences, the following four steps should help you plan the way to a successful digital lab setup:

1. Vision/strategy and goals.
2. Milestones.
3. Personnel and location.
4. Ensure interlocking.

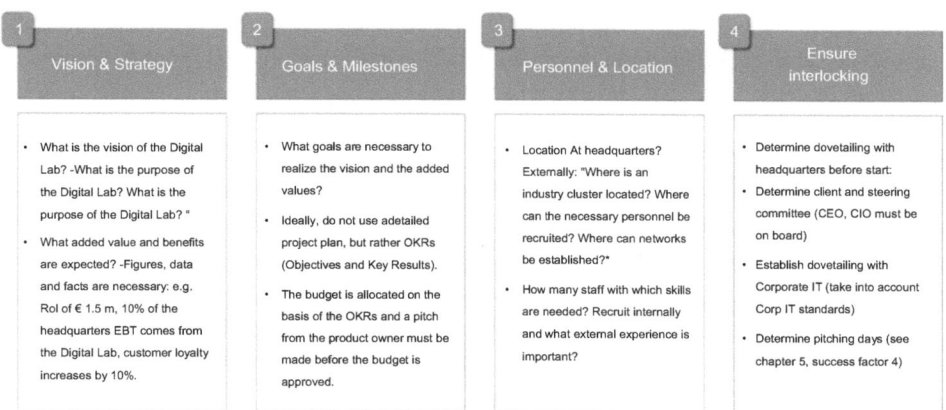

Fig. 3.17 The structure of a digital lab in four steps

Figure 3.17 uses a checklist to illustrate the four steps, including an example relating to the agricultural machinery manufacturing sector.

The Initial Situation

Until now, agricultural machinery manufacturers have almost exclusively sold their machines through dealers. However, digitalization in the form of platforms or market-places is now opening the door for manufacturers to sell their machines themselves. This has two weighty advantages: The margin that the dealer used to get remains with the manufacturer. The manufacturer has a direct contact to his end customer and can much better guess which optimizations are necessary on his product/machine. In addition, origi-nal spare parts can also be sold as an after-sales solution via such a marketplace or platform.

Since the development and provision of such a platform represents a challenge for the specialist departments involved internally, in particular IT, which is also currently unable to provide the appropriate resources and skills for this, it was decided to establish a digital lab for the design of the business model and the development and operation of this platform.

Step 1

The question of the vision or of the sense ("What are we doing this for?") presented in the first step thus refers to the "creation of our own platform for selling the machines as well as original spare parts." In concrete terms with figures, data, and facts, this means this platform increases the margin and thus the EBIT of the manufacturer by 7.5% due to the fact that it is sold directly and the previous margin of the dealer himself is retained. Of course, they do not want to alienate their dealers completely, so they are opening up this platform to dealers as well, but then with different margins than before, because the plat-form belongs to the manufacturer, who can determine the prices of the machine as well as the transaction costs. In addition, the digital lab will be used to develop contacts with start-ups and build up expertise in digital farming. This should ensure the company's competitive strength in the future by discovering and implementing future digital business models.

Step 2
This vision can now be broken down into the following goals (there should be a maximum of three to four goals):

Objective 1: Establishment of the digital lab and design of a business model for the platform including pricing models and necessary sales and marketing activities as well as make-or-buy strategy (which parts of the platform will be developed and operated in-house or outsourced to external parties)

Goal 2: Design and development of the platform according to agile methods (depending on the make-or-buy strategy, also negotiations with external partners and contract design including clean SLAs for the operation of the platform)

Goal 3: Go live including customer support and marketing activities as well as a well-planned and coordinated handover to the headquarters for the operation of the platform (depending on the make-or-buy strategy internally the headquarters or externally)

Objective 4: Development of further business models for the lab to secure the competitive strength of the parent company (e.g., screening and establishing contacts with start-ups from the industry, building up know-how on digital farming and related digital topics, derivation of digital business models for the parent company)

Step 3
The location issue in this example primarily addresses the issue of personnel recruitment, as this was the decisive bottleneck in the initial situation. Since the digital lab will not only be used for the design and development of the platform but also for networking with other start-ups and building know-how in digital topics (such as digital farming, connectivity services, etc.), a location in an existing ecosystem of many agribusiness start-ups makes sense. Nevertheless, the digital lab should not be too far away from the headquarters, as the operation of the platform will be taken over by the headquarters and thus a close relationship between the two needs to take place. The rather rural area of East Westphalia-Lippe (OWL) has been shortlisted, as well as Berlin. In terms of personnel recruitment and proximity to the headquarters, OWL is the winner, especially since the start-up scene for agribusiness is well worth seeing there for the development of networks and research on current topics related to digital farming.

During the staff question itself, the vision and goals of the digital lab were presented internally as part of a "pitching day." Every employee with an exciting idea and a business case was able to pitch his or her idea, and the three first place winners received a budget for the implementation of their idea in the digital lab and were released from their actual job as a product owner for 1 year and sent to the digital lab. This drew a lot of attention to the digital lab and started an internal application process that sent a lot of internal talent to the digital lab. It was important to the management that an IT architect and a manager from the executive board itself go to the digital lab and take on responsibility there. Thus, only two positions were needed to start the digital lab, which were recruited externally (an agile coach and a SCRUM master, as this knowledge and experience were not yet available internally).

Step 4

The integration and dovetailing of the new digital lab with the headquarters is a key success criterion. Much has already been gained through the internal recruitment of personnel in step 3. This is because the internally recruited digital lab employees will have a close exchange with their "old" colleagues and, above all, will be familiar with the existing IT landscape and its standards. This ensures that there is no overlap in development and that the apps of the digital lab fit into the IT architecture of the headquarters and can be seamlessly integrated into operations there. It is important not only to pay attention to IT but to include specialist departments such as service or after-sales in particular. After all, these departments will later have to be the hotline for end customers who have a problem with the platform. This requires planning with regard to a ticket system as well as shift planning for the employees. Close cooperation with purchasing and legal negotiations with external partners are just as important and contribute to the close cooperation between headquarters and digital lab.

3.4.4.3 Three Important Success Factors for a Digital Lab
Integration of the Parent Company and Close Cooperation
The biggest hurdle is that the lab is too detached from the mother ship. The positive results in the lab do not reach the parent company at all or cannot be adapted. There is rather an alienation and sometimes even competitive thinking. However, the goal should be to support the parent company with digital products and topics and not to compete. Figure 3.18 shows the differences in the work and thinking between a digital lab and a parent company. The interface between the two "worlds" is culture; if the two converge, this can only be achieved through curiosity and the acceptance of differences.

Another success factor for ensuring that the parent company and the digital lab do not drift apart or even come together in the first place can be the pitching of ideas. Figure 3.19 shows an example of how the parent company can organize such pitching days so that both worlds can be brought closer together. This is because joint thinking both in the digital lab and in the parent company gives birth to joint ideas, which are then jointly accompanied and developed through development to series maturity.

Digital Tools and Developments from the Lab Must Be Able to Be Operated by Corporate IT
The worst thing that can happen: The lab develops successful software products, but the internal IT cannot operate and further develop them, simply because the platform or the

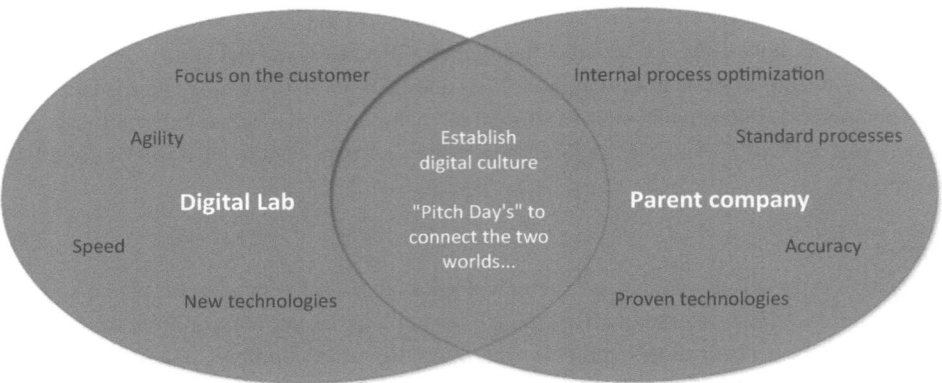

Fig. 3.18 Digital lab versus parent company

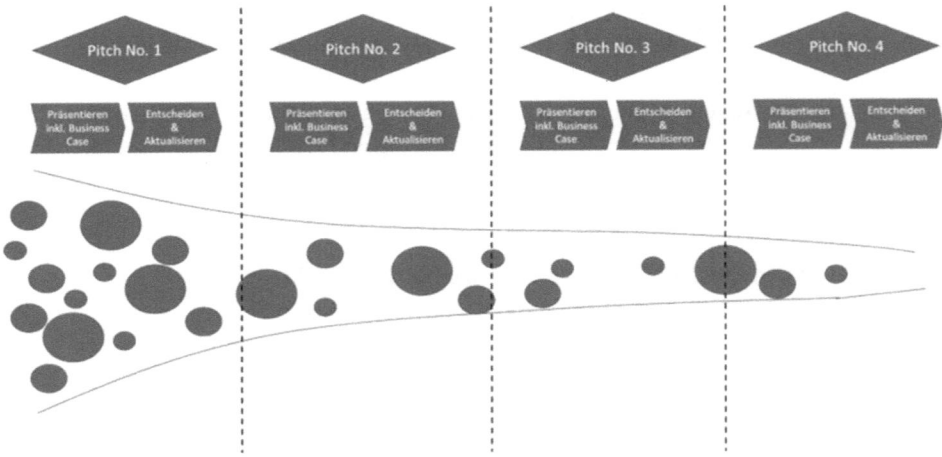

Fig. 3.19 Procedure: pitching ideas and product developments

internal knowledge is missing. This leads to a lot of frustration on both sides. Therefore, the CIO of the headquarters must work together with the lab managers to define the common platforms, programming languages, and standards regarding hardware and software. IT should therefore also provide the digital infrastructure platform.

No or Only Rudimentary Cost and Time Planning as Well as Poor Requirements Management
Many topics or projects are simply started in the lab without actually checking to what extent they are economical and offer the customer or the target group a real benefit. Often

it is not clear who from the management of the parent company is behind it (sponsor or client is missing). Simple rules from project management are often not lived in the lab. In addition, clear requirements for the software or product to be developed are often missing. The "excuse" that this is not needed for a minimum viable product (MVP) and in an agile environment is simply not true. All these facts together often lead to half-cooked products or results, and the awakening in reality is unfortunately often great.

3.4.5 Tip from the Field: When and Where Do Agile Approaches Make Sense?

In order to be able to answer the question about the use of agile methods, it makes sense to look at the different "needs" of IT systems. Gartner differentiates between three different levels of IT systems (Table 3.3).

Based on the three different levels of IT systems, it quickly becomes clear when and where agile methods really make sense and create efficiency in application development.

Table 3.3 The three levels of IT systems

Attributes	Systems of record	Systems of differentiation	Systems of innovation
Pace of change	Slow, infrequent, and incremental. Changes every 6–12 months	Moderate and more frequent. Configurability is key. Changes every 3–6 months	Rapid, very frequent, and ad hoc. "Throwaway" customization. Changes weekly, sometimes daily
Lifetime	10+ years	1–3 years	0 to 12 months
Planning horizon	7+ years	1–3 years	Up to 6 months
Governance model	Formal and global	Responsive and business-led	Flexible and ad hoc
Stakeholders/ownership	High business executive engagement; alignment between business and IT strategy. Low end-user engagement and formal handover from the business to IT	High business executive engagement, but driven by lines of business. Moderate end-user engagement, with the business engaging on hot spots and IT filling the gaps	Moderate business executive engagement, with some sponsored and under the radar; tactical. High end-user engagement, often through business users or even circumventing IT
Architecture	Large, modular design dominated by formal, upfront blueprinting phase	Service-oriented architecture (SOA) and cloud-based, with a mix of service consumers and producers	Lightweight and emergent, predominantly service consumers. Mobile and cloud-dominated

Source: According to Gartner [7]

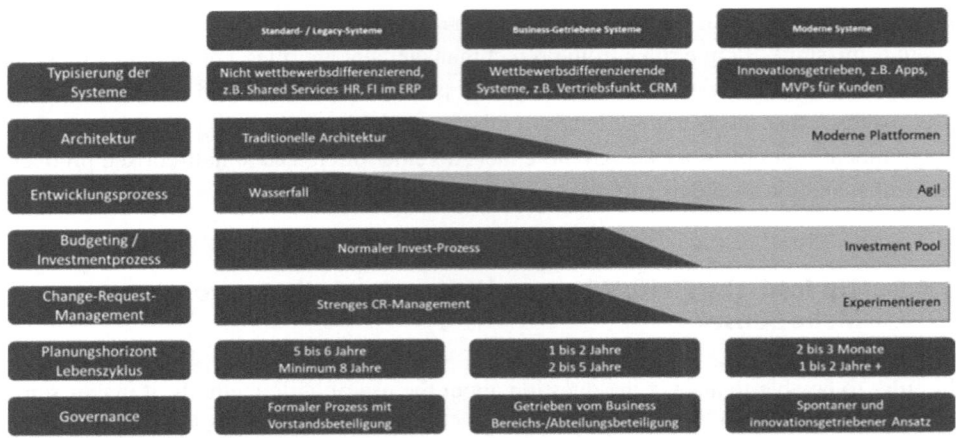

Fig. 3.20 Different organizational procedures depending on the system

A good overview of this is provided in Fig. 3.20. Based on the IT system used, it is differentiated which type of development process, budget, or change request management process should be used. Here it also becomes clear that for modern IT systems (for Gartner, these are the "Systems of Innovation"), the agile methods make sense and are almost irreplaceable. Whereas the legacy systems and relatively rigid ERP systems (with Gartner the so-called "Systems of Record") rather the traditional waterfall model leads to success. Therefore, agile approaches such as sprints can definitely be used in the waterfall model as well.

As a final tip from the field, I would like to suggest two things that will quickly help you become agile without immediately implementing all sorts of methods and best practices:

Speed: What keeps you from "finishing"? What can be turned off so you can be focused and productive on your topic? If you notice that you are getting distracted, immediately switch back to productive mode. You must always keep the goal in mind and just get things done.

Consistency: To stay in "finish mode," you need consistency. You need to turn down other things and projects. You need to be able to concentrate fully on one thing and thus "alienate" other requesters or put them off until later. You need to cancel meetings and "fend off" phone calls and do it consistently. Then you will achieve your goal in the most "agile" way possible.

3.5   The Process Organization as an Interface to the Specialist Departments

Trailer
IT can never be successful on its own – process organization shows how the business departments can be closely involved in the joint work.

In order for the IT organization to be truly capable of delivering, the interface to the business departments must be clearly regulated. Ideally, this is done at the process level and thus within the framework of a process organization.

Furthermore, it must be clear in this interface who assumes which responsibilities. This includes the roles of the process owners and experts as well as key users on the business side and their counterparts on the IT side. These are described in detail below.

3.5.1   The Question of the Responsibility of a Process Organization

It should also be noted at this point that such a process organization is not founded or brought into being by the departments, since they only consider their processes and thus the overall view of all processes of the company never arises. The management or the board of directors is usually not on the process level, but rather in the functional framework of the pure organizational structure, i.e., the organizational chart. Then, in manufacturing companies, there is also quality management, which, according to various norms and standards, e.g., ISO 9001, demands that every process must be planned, controlled, monitored, and improved. However, this is rather the view on the correctness of the processes in the sense of audits and not the view on the real efficiency, which has to be mapped in IT systems afterward.

Therefore, it is usually the CIO's responsibility to set up such a process organization together with the management. Particularly in the case of upcoming ERP implementations or other major projects, the process organization is the ideal link between IT and the business department, especially to make it clear that such projects are not IT projects, but projects of the entire company in which the processes are optimized.

3.5.2   The Three Levels of Requirements Management

Before explaining exactly how a process organization is set up, it makes sense to take a closer look at what the roles of the process organization are responsible for and what their tasks are.

There are three levels of the requirements management process, shown in Fig. 3.21:

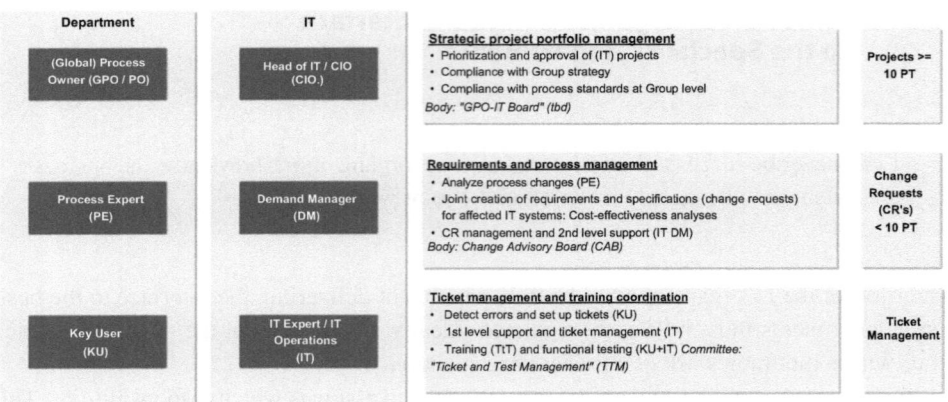

Fig. 3.21 The three levels of the requirements management process

- *Strategic project portfolio management*: At this level, the CIO and the respective process owner prioritize large projects with more than 10 person-days (this can be individually adjusted depending on the company) and release them as required. This level is important because it ensures that each project complies with the process standards and the group strategy. It makes sense for this coordination to take place regularly in a defined framework and committee.
- *Requirements and process management*: This is the typical change request management (CR management) cycle, which takes place at the level of the process experts on the business side and the requirements or demand manager on the IT side. It primarily involves the joint creation of specifications and concepts for process changes and optimizations in day-to-day business. In addition, second level support takes place here. The typical body for this exchange is the regularly held CR management board.
- *Ticket management*: This is the level at which the key users on the business side work together with the IT experts. The key users have the task of identifying errors in the IT systems, formulating them, and entering them into the ticket system. On the IT side, the key user is responsible for first level support, ticket management, and performing functional tests in order to re-provide the fixed errors and problems in the IT systems. The role profile of the key user also includes the topic of education and training of the users assigned to him.

This construct creates the basis for establishing a process organization that serves as an interface between the business departments and IT.

3.5.3   Important Roles in the Process Organization

Before the process organization is finally set up, the roles must first be clarified. Figures 3.22 and 3.23 show the total of six roles that are necessary for a functioning process organization; these are in detail:

At the department level:

- Key user.
- Process expert.
- Process owner.
- Global process owner (for international companies).

At the IT level:

- Demand manager or account manager.
- IT expert.

The role descriptions deliberately include the topics "handover points" and "out of scope." This serves to clearly regulate who takes over which topics or not.

Furthermore, it should be mentioned that the role of the global process owner can only be found in companies that operate internationally and have significant production or sales locations abroad. In this case, it makes sense that one role is responsible for the global compliance with standards regarding processes and strategy. For each location, company, or country, there is then a separate process owner for the respective process, who can, however, also be the global process owner in a personal union.

	Globaler Prozessverantwortlicher (GPO)	Prozessverantwortlicher (PO)	Prozessexperte (PE)
Rolle	• Weltweite Gesamtverantwortung für den jeweiligen E2E-Prozess	• Verantwortung für den jeweiligen E2E-Prozess • Budget-Verantwortung für den jeweiligen E2E-Prozess in der Gesellschaft	• Expertenwissen für alle Prozesse innerhalb des jeweiligen E2E-Prozesses • Hauptansprechpartner der zugeordneten Key User
Aufgaben	• Sorgt für die Einhaltung der Unternehmensstrategie • Ist verantwortlich für die Schaffung und Einhaltung von Standards auf globaler Ebene • Abstimmung und Harmonisierung von Prozessen mit den anderen Globalen Prozessverantwortlichen (GPO's)	• Analyse von Prozessveränderungen und deren Auswirkungen • Change Management für Prozessänderungen • Definieren Ziele und KPI's für Prozesse • Abstimmung und Harmonisierung mit den Process Ownern der anderen E2E-Prozesse	• Definition und Beschreibung der fachlichen Anforderungen (Lastenheft) für neue Prozesse oder Prozessänderungen (Change Requests) • Erstellung von Business Cases und Wirtschaftlichkeitsrechnungen • Überwachung von Funktionstests • Freigabe der getesteten Change Requests
Übergabe-punkte	• Berichtet gegenüber der Geschäftsführung der Holding	• Freigabe der Lastenhefte und Change Requests	• Abstimmung und Vorlage zur Freigabe an den Process Owner für neue Prozesse oder Prozessänderungen
Out-of-Scope		• Keine Modellierung	• Keine Testdurchführung (Tests werden von Key Usern durchgeführt)

Fig. 3.22 The roles in the process organization Part I

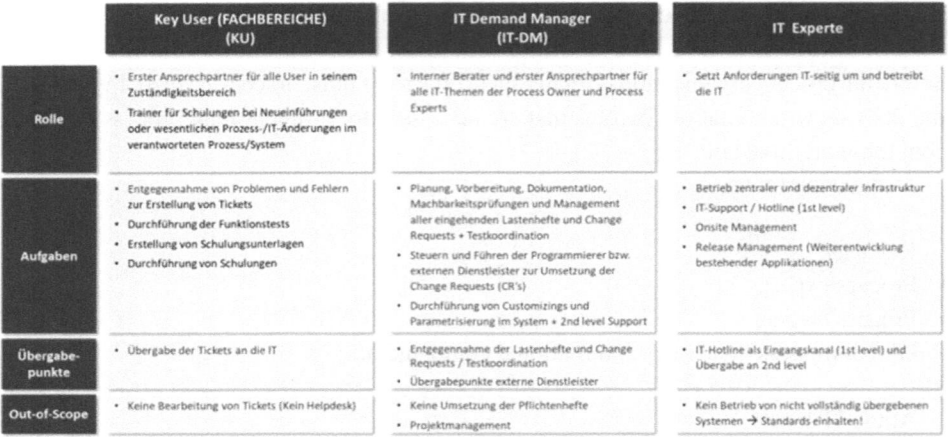

Fig. 3.23   The roles in the process organization Part II

3.5.4   Establishment of a Process Organization

The development of a process organization can be done in three steps.

3.5.4.1 Step 1: Define End-to-End Processes

A good process organization is ideally oriented toward the so-called end-to-end processes. These have the advantage that thinking and acting are actually interdepartmental and inter-departmental. This means, for example, that in the end-to-end process "Order-to-Ship," sales, production, and logistics are equally involved in the process. Therefore, it should be avoided to use the often typical organizational plan for a process organization. An over-view of typical end-to-end processes with an example of added value in an ERP project can be found in Fig. 3.24.

So the task now is to define the end-to-end processes that are essential for your com-pany and to coordinate these with the management and the department heads.

In a manufacturing company, for example, this might look like Table 3.4:

3.5.4.2 Step 2: Distribute the Roles

The next step is to assign the appropriate roles to the appropriate people per end-to-end process as shown in Sect. 3.5.2 (see Fig. 3.25).

The following special features must be observed:

- Not everywhere a split in process responsibility is needed. And this division can be dif-ferent. For example, in the end-to-end process P2S (Plan-to-Ship), it makes sense to divide by plant. On the other hand, in the case of financial and personnel processes, as well as in the case of sales, it makes sense to divide by region (in this example, the

End-to-End Business process	Description	Possible added value through a new ERP
Idea for product	from the idea or the customer's request to the finished product (Product management. Technical development - R&D) -	• Increase in Time-to-Market or Product-to-Market by x%. • Increase of process efficiency in the TE by x% -> thus increase of product safety by y%. • Customer loyalty increases by x% due to faster and better fulfilment of customer requirements
Prospect to customer	From customer interest (lead) to customer (marketing & sales)	More of a CRM topic, but often plays a role in ERP topics. • A more efficient customer approach is made possible • Customer attractiveness increases by x% through multi-channel marketing • More efficient master data maintenance: No duplication of customers, more customer details, etc. -> leads to more efficient customer approaches, thus to more appreciation by customers and higher customer loyalty
Order to delivery	From customer order to delivery to the customer (sales, production, logistics)	• Increase of the degree of automation by 25%, thus cost savings of y TEm • Predictive maintenance can reduce the usual machine downtime to a minimum (= machine utilization close to 100%) and maintenance can plan highly efficiently. • Intelligent warehouse management leads to optimised internal warehouse management and means short delivery routes and thus delivery times for the customer. This increases customer loyalty by 20%.
Service requirement for problem solving	From reporting a fault or problem of a customer to his Solution (Sales, After Sales, (QM), TE, Product Management)	• Optimized customer communication, reduced response time to the customer and errors can be solved much faster → Customer attractiveness increases by x%. • Constant transparency and reports on number of defects, frequency, etc. → Feedback for product improvement (product benefit increases by y%) and customer satisfaction increases by x%.

Fig. 3.24 End-to-end processes at a glance (exemplary)

Table 3.4 End-to-end processes (example for a manufacturing company)

End-to-end process	Description
P2S: Plan-to-ship	From initial requirements planning to shipment to the customer
	Areas involved: Sales/disposition, production, supply chain, logistics, QA
D2D: Design-to-deploy	From the initial inquiry until the product is ready for production (including modification service, sampling, and phasing out of the product)
	Involved areas: Technical development/project planning, production planning, QM
S2P: Source-to-pay	Purchasing processes from the procurement strategy to the payment of the supplier invoice
	Involved areas: Purchasing, finance, controlling
C2C: Contract-to-cash	Sales processes from sales strategy to receipt of payment and handling of returns
	Involved areas: Sales, finance, controlling, supply chain management, QM/QS
R2R: Record-to-report	Financial processes and cash management from budgeting/planning to accounting and reporting
H2R: Hire-to-retire	Personnel processes from recruitment to departure
	Areas involved: Human resources, marketing, finance

Geschäftsprozess (Ende-zu-Ende)	Global Process Owner	Aufteilung	Process Owner	Process Experts	Key User	IT Demand Manager
P2S: Plan to Ship	Peter Produktion	Deutschland: Werk Nürnberg	Peter Produktion	Hans Transport (Halle 1+2), Friedrich Produktion (Halle 4)	Max Muster (Halle 1), Max Mester (Halle 2), Max Master (Halle 4)	Markus Supp (SAP eWM), Friedrich Log (SAP PP), Friedel Prod (MES)
		USA: Werk Chicago	Marc Prodi	George Supply (Plant 1), Jimmy Prod (Plant 2)	George Supply (Plant 1), Jimmy Prod (Plant 2)	Markus Supp (SAP eWM), Friedrich Log (SAP PP), Friedel Prod (MES), Albert (MES)
		China: Werk Shanghai	Bin Bin	Bin Bin	Chung Supply	Markus Supp (SAP eWM), Friedrich Log (SAP PP), Friedel Prod (MES)
D2D: Design to Deploy	Frank Tüftel		Frank Tüftel	Hans Bemuster	Hansi Projektier	Friedrich Coder
S2P: Source to Pay	Max Verhandel		Max Verhandel	Franz Sorce	Franz Sorce	Wilhelm Agilus (SAP MM)
C2C: Contract to Cash	Felix Geschäftemacher	Region Europa	Felix Geschäftemacher	Hannes Verkauf	Hannes Verkauf	Kim Custom (Salesforce)
		Region Amerika	Donald Sales	Donald Sales	Donald Sales	Kim Custom (Salesforce), Jimmy (eigenes CRM)
		Region Asien	Felix Geschäftemacher (i.PU)	Ed Chung	Ed Chung	Kim Custom (Salesforce)
R2R: Record to Report	Hans Pfenningfuchser	Region Europa	Hans Pfenningfuchser			Hans Friedrich Gold (SAP FI), Emelie Kontroletti (SAP CO)
		Region Amerika	Mason Fin	Mason Fin	Ethan Control	
		Region Asien	Sun Sun	Sun Sun	Bao Bang	
H2R: Hire to Retire	Paula Personalis	Region Europa	Paula Personalis	Carolina Humana	Carolina Humana	Michael Personalis (SuccessFactors)
		Region Amerika	Jim Hen	Jimmy Plu	Jimmy Plu	Michael Personalis (SuccessFactors)
		Region Asien	Chan Chang	Chan Chang	Chan Chang	Michael Personalis (SuccessFactors)

Fig. 3.25 Structure of a process organization (exemplified by a manufacturing company)

regions Europe, America, and Asia). The processes D2D and S2P do not need to be divided, as they are managed centrally from the headquarters.

- Global process owner and process owner are often the same, at least for one region (e.g., the German process owner is also the globally responsible process owner).
- In the case of the process experts, a further subdivision can result. This granularity makes sense, for example, in the division according to halls, if different products with different processes are manufactured in the halls or plants.

- At the level of the IT demand manager, differentiation is then often no longer made according to processes, but instead the processes are assigned to the IT systems required for them. In the P2S (Plan-to-Ship) process, for example, these are the SAP modules PP (Production Planning), eWM (extended Warehouse Management), and an MES. This then officially marries the process to the IT system.

3.5.4.3 Step 3: "Marrying" the IT Organization and the Process Organization

After the roles have been clearly defined, the next step is to link the IT organization with the process organization. As shown in Fig. 3.26, the IT organization at the level of the "PLAN" area is linked to the end-to-end process owners at the business unit level. These IT teams from the "PLAN" are in turn linked to the BUILD team, each of which contains and is responsible for the IT systems required for the end-to-end process. The "RUN" area in the form of "Global IT Operations" is encapsulated from this, as these must be provided independently of the end-to-end processes for the entire company.

The distribution of tasks in the case of a requirement or process change in the department looks as follows:

At the business level, the process changes are identified in the process organization and then discussed with the PLAN team from IT. Together with the build colleague and the process owners, they draft a requirements specification or a concept (or, according to the agile approach, a user story). This is then developed in the build team and functionally tested by the process owners. When approved by the process owner, the function is run in the appropriate IT system by RUN (Global IT Operations). This is a simplified process representation, but for the general representation of the flow between IT and process organization, this should suffice for the time being.

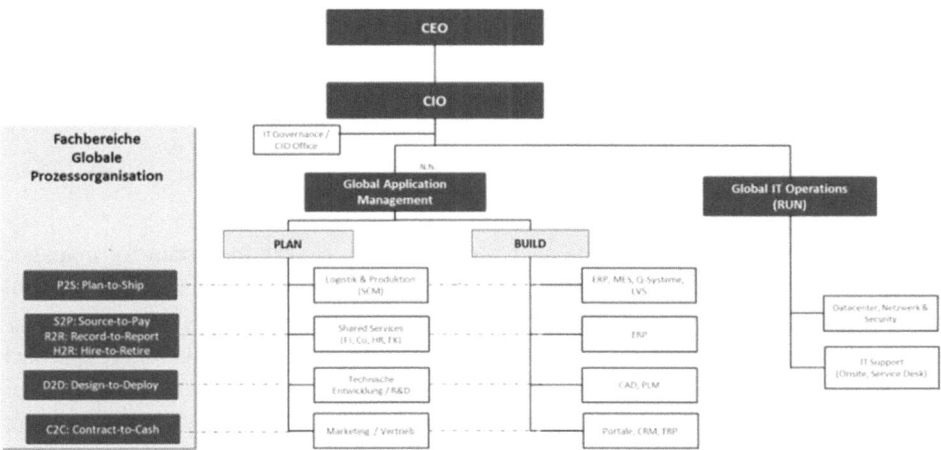

Fig. 3.26 "Marrying" the IT and process organization

In the exemplary Fig. 3.26, the assignment and linkage for the six end-to-end processes look as follows:

- The end-to-end process P2S (Plan-to-Ship) is linked with the team "Logistics and Production" on the IT side and then again with the team Build, which is responsible for the required IT systems for this end-to-end process. P2S is an extensive process block, so there are also four IT systems in the minimum. In this example, these are the IT systems ERP, Q systems, a WMS (warehouse management system), and an MES (manufacturing execution system), all of which support the P2S processes.
- The end-to-end processes S2P (Source-to-Pay), R2R (Record-to-Report), and H2R (Hire-to-Retire) are a special feature. These are all assigned to one team in IT under the heading "Shared Services." The background for this lies in common system uses, because these processes are typical ERP processes that are all found in the same system. Therefore, they have been "combined" on the IT side. Of course, it is still important that the PLAN team in IT has the expertise for all three end-to-end processes so that communication and concept creation can run smoothly.
- The end-to-end process D2D (Design-to-Deploy) is linked on the IT or PLAN side with the "Technical Development/R&D" team, which is then responsible for the necessary IT systems such as a PLM or CAD system in the build area.
- The end-to-end process C2C (Contract-to-Cash) is linked to "Marketing/Sales" on the plan side, in order to support the IT systems in the build part CRM and ERP and portals there.

3.5.4.4 Step 4: Formally Introduce the Process Organization

In order for the process organization to develop its full power, it must first be adopted by the management. And then, above all, communication and training are important.

The primary goal is to train all process owners as well as experts, key users, and IT demand managers in their new roles with the following content:

- What are the tasks and responsibilities?
- What interfaces do I have with the other roles?
- How does the "interaction" between the roles work (see Sect. 3.5.4.2)?
- How much time does the role require (in which project phase)?

The question of how much time such a role requires is very important for managers, because in projects, such as an ERP implementation, process managers are almost 100% busy, depending on the project phase. To stay with the ERP implementation example: In a larger medium-sized company with about 2000 employees and a greenfield approach, such an ERP implementation can take as long as 5 years. During these 5 years, not every process expert is 100% occupied with the ERP project, but in peak phases, such as before the go live and during training courses and the business blueprint phase, they certainly are. This is not clear to many managers, and therefore such projects are often very tough in their execution.

In day-to-day business, when no major projects are pending, a process expert is mainly concerned with process changes that are then introduced into the IT systems in the usual CR way (as a change request). This should be routine and takes up between 20% and 50% of his time, depending on the process optimization potential.

3.6   Summary and Plea for a Modern IT Organization

When it comes to the topic of designing an IT organization, the three questions formulated in accordance with Malik [8] apply, which must be taken into account as maxims for action for the management and the CIO when (re)designing an IT organization:

1. How must an IT organization be designed so that what the customer pays us for is at the center of attention and cannot disappear from there?
2. How does an IT organization have to be designed so that what we pay our IT staff to do can actually be done by them?
3. How must an IT organization be designed so that what the CIO and IT management are paid to do can actually be done by them?

Point 1 sounds logical and easy, and of course the business departments are the focus. As IT, you are at least a service provider if you have a modern setup. But it is often very difficult, especially for an IT organization, to recognize what the customer is paying IT for. First of all, the question arises: "Who exactly is our customer?" Is it top management in the sense of the executive team or the board of directors, is it the owner or shareholder of the company, or is it the business departments and perhaps even the end customers? The answer to this question alone is very important, however, because between all the possible customers mentioned, there are very likely to be very different views of what constitutes "good" or the "right" IT. IT is usually not spun off as an independent company in the form of a GmbH (limited liability company), for example, but rather an internal organization that receives a budget from the management, and for the various IT projects, there should ideally always be a client and sponsor who pays for the project. This is usually from the business department. In some cases, IT becomes a product, for example, it is also integrated into the car and is therefore important for the end customer. These are completely different requirements than for internal customers. So it is very difficult to reconcile all these different interests and intentions of the possible customers.

Therefore, particularly with regard to the third point, it must be very clearly defined by the management or the board of directors what IT and the CIO stand for. It is important that the organization is designed in such a way that the CIO and IT management do not get lost in the day-to-day business but can really develop IT with a bird's-eye view. This is described in detail in this book in Sect. 4.4.9, which describes the role identification of IT and the CIO in the company.

References

1. *Zarnekow, Brenner, Grohmann*: Informationsmanagement: Konzepte und Strategien für die Praxis, 1. Auflage, dpunkt.Verlag, 2004.
2. *Zarnekow, Brenner, Pilgram*: Integriertes Informationsmanagement, 1. Auflager, Springer, 2005.
3. *Urbach, Ahlemann*: (2017). Die IT-Organisation im Wandel: Implikationen der Digitalisierung für das IT-Management. HMD Praxis der Wirtschaftsinformatik. 54. 300–312.
4. *Drucker, Peter F.*: "Management's New Paradigm", http://www.mit.edu/~mbarker/ideas/drucker.html, MIT, abgerufen am 30.12.2019.
5. *Ellermann, Horst*: "BMW-CIO hält Bimodal IT für einen Irrweg", abgerufen am 28.12.2019, https://www.cio.de/a/bmw-cio-haelt-bimodal-it-fuer-einen-irrweg,3562374
6. *Anderson, David J.*: "Kanban: Evolutionäres Change Management für IT-Organisationen", 1. Auflage, dpunkt, 2011.
7. *Gartner: Mary Mesaglio, Matthew Hotel*: "Pace-Layered Application Strategy and IT Organizational Design: How to Structure the Application Team for Success", https://www.gartner.com/binaries/content/assets/events/keywords/applications/apn30/pace-layered-applications-research-report.pdf, abgerufen am 07.01.2020.
8. *Malik, Fredmund*: Führen Leisten Leben, 6. Auflage, Campus Verlag, 2006.

The Process Organization of IT: Which IT Processes and Structures Does a Modern and Lean IT Organization of the Future Need?

4

Abstract

In the context of the process organization of an IT, the question is "What is to be done when and in what order?". It is about the internal processes in IT, i.e., the IT processes.

4.1 IT Governance as a Framework for IT Process Organization

At this point, one automatically comes to the topic of "IT governance." Indeed, IT governance describes the processes and organizational structures that ensure that IT supports the corporate strategy and goals (adapted from [1]). In this context, two goals are important for IT governance:

- The creation of enterprise value.
- The minimization of IT risks.

To achieve these goals, IT governance relies on the following frameworks, which are now standardized and internationally accepted:

- Corporate governance standard: COSO, ISO/IEC 38500:2008.
- Overarching standard and link to corporate governance: COBIT (Control Objectives for Information and Related Technology).
- Implementation of IT service management: ISO 20000, ITIL (Information Technology Infrastructure Library).
- Information security: ISO/IEC 2700x and IT-Grundschutz Catalogues.
- Project management: PMBOK, ICB, and PRINCE2.

© The Author(s), under exclusive license to Springer Fachmedien Wiesbaden
GmbH, part of Springer Nature 2024
V. Johanning, *Organization and Management of IT*,
https://doi.org/10.1007/978-3-658-39572-8_4

- Architecture: TOGAF.
- System development: TickIT and CMMI.

For the design of an IT process organization, two frameworks are essentially of greater importance. These are COBIT and ITIL. These are therefore presented in more detail below and examined for practical usability.

4.2   Overview of Common Frameworks for IT Process Organization

4.2.1   COBIT as a Possible Reference Model for the IT Process Organization

4.2.1.1 Definition and Objective of COBIT

COBIT was an abbreviation for "Control Objectives for Information and Related Technology" until version 4.1. In the current version 5.0, COBIT is only used as an acronym.

The publisher and developer of this COBIT framework is the international association of IT auditors called ISACA ("Information Systems Audit and Control Association"). In the original 1996 version, it was intended as a tool for standardized IT reviews and IT audits. In addition, it is used as a model for ensuring compliance with legal requirements.

In the meantime, it has also become a widespread standard in large companies, at least in large parts. There, it primarily continues to serve to ensure compliance regulations. In addition, it often serves as a link between IT-specific frameworks such as ITIL and the model for general compliance with corporate governance COSO.

4.2.1.2 The Structure and Functioning of COBIT

According to ISACA [1], the five fundamental principles for governance and management of enterprise IT are as follows (Fig. 4.1):

- Meeting the requirements of stakeholders.
- Coverage of the entire company.
- Application of a single, integrated framework.
- Enabling a holistic approach.
- Distinction between governance and management.

The COBIT 5 process reference model defines 37 processes grouped into 5 domains, including 1 governance domain (EDM) and 4 management domains (APO, BAI, DSS, and MEA), also referred to as PBRM (Plan, Build, Run, and Monitor).

These processes can be roughly contrasted with the 26 processes from ITIL 2011, which are grouped into the 5 modules of Service Strategy (SS), Service Design (SD),

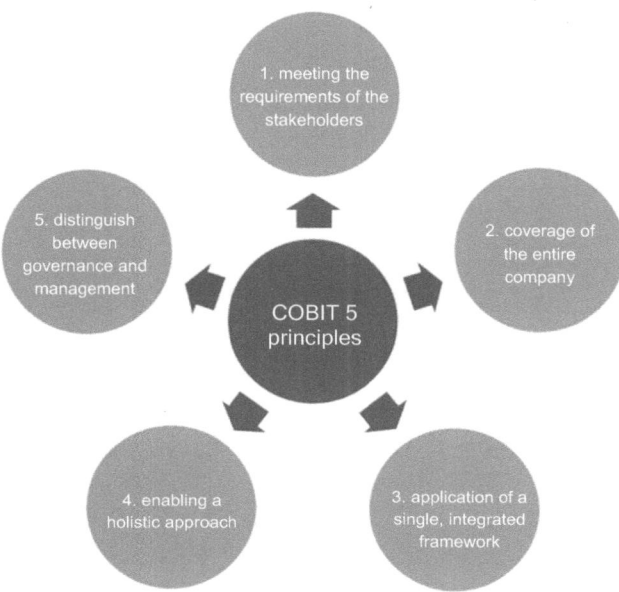

Fig. 4.1 COBIT 5 principles

Service Transition (ST), Service Operation (SO), and Continual Service Improvement (CSI) [2].

The 37 COBIT 5 processes are mapped in Fig. 4.2 as "Processes for Governance of Enterprise IT" and are structured as follows [1]:

- EDM – Evaluate, Direct, and Monitor.
  - EDM01 Ensure the establishment and maintenance of the governance framework.
  - EDM02 Ensure delivery of value contributions.
  - EDM03 Ensure risk optimization.
  - EDM04 Ensure resource optimization.
  - EDM05 Ensure transparency toward stakeholders.
- APO – Align, Plan, and Organize.
  - APO01 Managing the IT management framework.
  - APO02 Managing the strategy.
  - APO03 Managing enterprise architecture.
  - APO04 Managing innovation.
  - APO05 Managing the portfolio.
  - APO06 Managing budget and costs.
  - APO07 Managing personnel.
  - APO08 Managing relationships.
  - APO09 Managing service agreements.

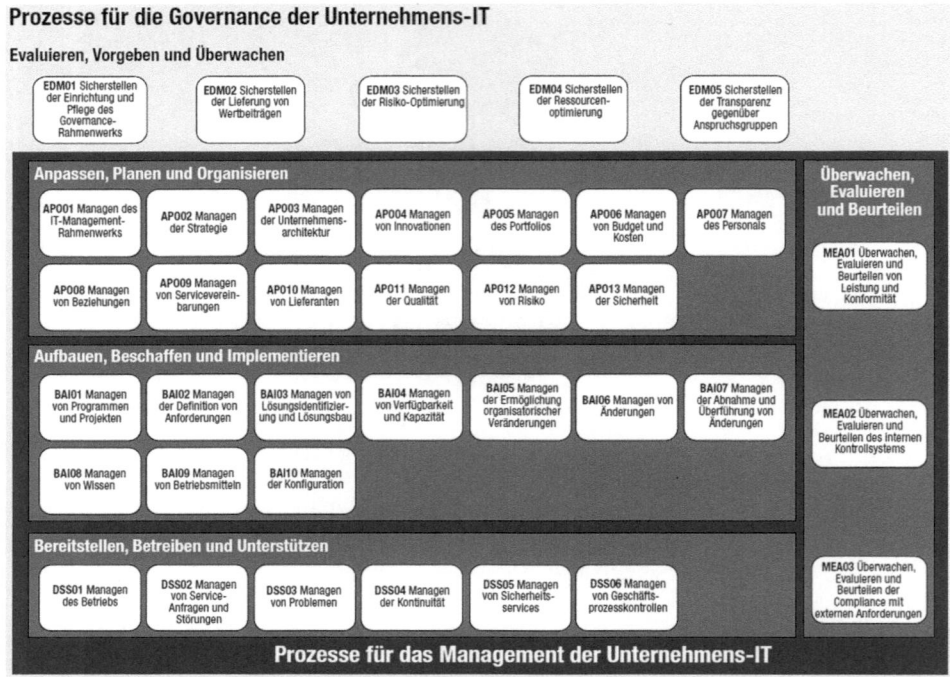

Fig. 4.2 Processes for the governance of corporate IT

- – APO10 Managing suppliers.
- – APO11 Managing quality.
- – APO12 Managing risk.
- – APO13 Managing security.
- • BAI – Build, Acquire, and Implement.
  - – BAI01 Managing programs and projects.
  - – BAI02 Managing the definition of requirements.
  - – BAI03 Managing solution identification and solution construction.
  - – BAI04 Managing availability and capacity.
  - – BAI05 Managing the enabling of organizational change.
  - – BAI06 Changing management.
  - – BAI07 Managing acceptance and transfer of changes.
  - – BAI08 Managing knowledge.
  - – BAI09 Managing operating resources.
  - – BAI10 Managing configuration.
- • DSS – Deliver, Service, and Support.
  - – DSS01 Managing the operation.
  - – DSS02 Managing service requests and faults.
  - – DSS03 Managing problems.

- – DSS04 Managing continuity.
- – DSS05 Managing security services.
- – DSS06 Managing business process controls.
- MEA – Monitor, Evaluate, and Assess.
  - – MEA01 Monitor, evaluate, and assess performance and compliance.
  - – MEA02 Monitor, evaluate, and assess the internal control system.
  - – MEA03 Monitor, evaluate, and assess compliance with external requirements.

4.2.2   ITIL as a Framework for the Implementation of IT Service Management Standards

4.2.2.1 Definition and Objective of ITIL

ITIL is the abbreviation for "Information Technology Infrastructure Library" and contains a collection of predefined processes as well as functions and roles for IT service management.

It has established itself as a quasi-standard for the process design of IT operations and infrastructure departments of medium-sized companies and corporations.

ITIL was developed in the 1980s by the Central Computer and Telecommunications Agency (CCTA), until 2010 Office of Government Commerce (OGC) and now Cabinet Office, part of Her Majesty's Government (HMG), a government agency in the UK.

In the current version, ITIL version 4 has been published on February 18, 2019. Since 2014, the publisher and owner of the complete ITIL framework has been AXELOS. AXELOS Ltd. is a joint venture established by the UK Government and Capita to develop, manage, and apply best practice qualifications formerly owned by the Office of Government Commerce. It operates under the brand "AXELOS – Global Best Practice Solutions" at www.axelos.com. AXELOS is also the owner of PRINCE2, another well-known standard for IT project management in IT circles.

4.2.2.2 Overview of ITIL Management Practices

The current version ITIL v4 contains 4 dimensions of service management as well as 34 so-called management practices. The 34 management practices are of great interest for the consideration in this book with regard to the IT process organization. These are divided into three areas (general management practices, service management practices, and "technical management practices") and look as follows according to AXELOS [3]:

General Management Practices
- Strategy management.
- Portfolio management.
- Architecture management.
- Service financial management.
- Workforce and talent management.

- Continual improvement.
- Measurement and reporting.
- Risk management.
- Information security management.
- Knowledge management.
- Organizational change management.
- Project management.
- Relationship management.
- Supplier management.

Service Management Practices
- Business analysis.
- Service catalogue management.
- Service design.
- Service level management.
- Availability management.
- Capacity and performance management.
- Service continuity management.
- Monitoring and event management.
- Service desk.
- Incident management.
- Service request management.
- Problem management.
- Release management.
- Change enablement.
- Service validation and testing.
- Service configuration management.
- IT asset management.

Technical Management Practices
- Deployment management.
- Infrastructure and platform management.
- Software development and management.

ITIL v4 thus offers a very comprehensive catalogue of predefined IT processes, especially for IT service management, but also for overarching processes that extend into the controlling and leading area of IT governance.

4.2.3   A Guide Through the Jungle of ITIL, COBIT, and Co: What Is Really Important for the CIO?

In addition to ITIL and COBIT, other frameworks can be used, but they always focus on a specific area of expertise or an IT process. This can be, for example, PRINCE2, also managed by AXELOS, which provides a quasi-standard for IT project management. For IT architecture, TOGAF is available as a quasi-standard.

For the IT manager, it sometimes becomes very confusing. Therefore, the decision as to which of the frameworks should now be used for which IT process is sometimes understandably very difficult.

Figure 4.3 shows an overview of all frameworks from the COBIT perspective. It also becomes clear that many frameworks only cover a very specific subarea and not the entire IT.

In this illustration, COBIT assumes the quasi-general standard over all other frameworks. However, as a CIO, this should be critically questioned.

Because COBIT was still developed from history and for IT auditors it still bears this signature, as it is very much aimed at measuring, regulating, and controlling. COBIT has also become very comprehensive and therefore very complex. As a CIO, you can quickly feel overwhelmed. And in fact, the question arises as to how an IT manager is supposed to fully understand COBIT and thus be able to apply it in a meaningful way.

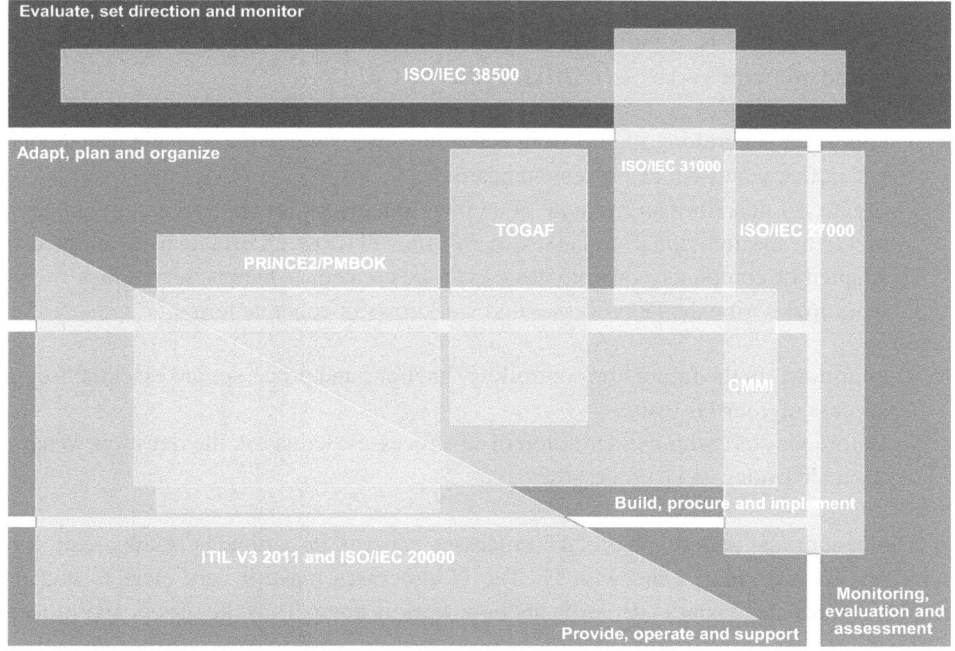

Fig. 4.3 Coverage of other standards and frameworks by COBIT 5

From the author's point of view, a full COBIT implementation only makes sense for companies that have regulations and compliance requirements from, e.g., SOX (Sarbanes-Oxley Act) or SAS-70, or other high regulatory requirements. For all other companies, it might even be a hindrance to have to adhere to these very concrete IT processes.

ITIL has also grown strongly over the years, and with version 4, an attempt has been made to incorporate the tendencies toward agile thinking and action so as not to miss the train of time. However, in contrast to COBIT, ITIL is more practical in some parts, and only individual IT processes can be used and introduced relatively quickly. This is especially helpful for small- and medium-sized companies. It is not necessary to start a large project for the introduction of a framework, but a corresponding IT process can be added or changed at any time.

Overall, it can be said that ITIL and COBIT complement each other quite well: ITIL helps to build processes, strategies, and services, and COBIT ensures that what has been built is compliant with rules and strategy.

The conclusion from the author's point of view is therefore use the two frameworks as a kind of toolbox. Take a look and see what can or should be used sensibly in your company.

The following section will help you to do this, in which IT processes are proposed for practical use within the framework of seven groups.

4.3   Your Own IT Framework

Your IT organization is as individual as your company: Not everything fits into the presented standard frameworks like COBIT, ITIL, and Co.

▶   **Important** Therefore, the tip from practice is use suitable parts of the frameworks and define your own IT process standard.
Figure 4.4 describes an example of an own framework for the process organization of IT. In the individual processes, parts from ITIL or COBIT can be adopted or adapted or completely own processes can be created. It merely serves as a framework to describe the IT processes and workflows in concrete terms.

▶   **Important** In the future, the controlling functions and processes are essential for the success of your IT-Team.
Before we start with the definition of IT processes, let us ask the question: What is the added value of IT processes?

The benefit and added value of IT processes consists in particular in the creation of standards for working in and with IT. The IT processes make it very clear to both IT employees and the business departments how work is done. Thus, key users and process owners know exactly how IT works, where interfaces to IT are, and how cooperation works. Within IT, in addition to transparency, it also serves to create quality through standard processes. And last but not least, it is a very helpful documentation for internal audits or preparation for certifications.

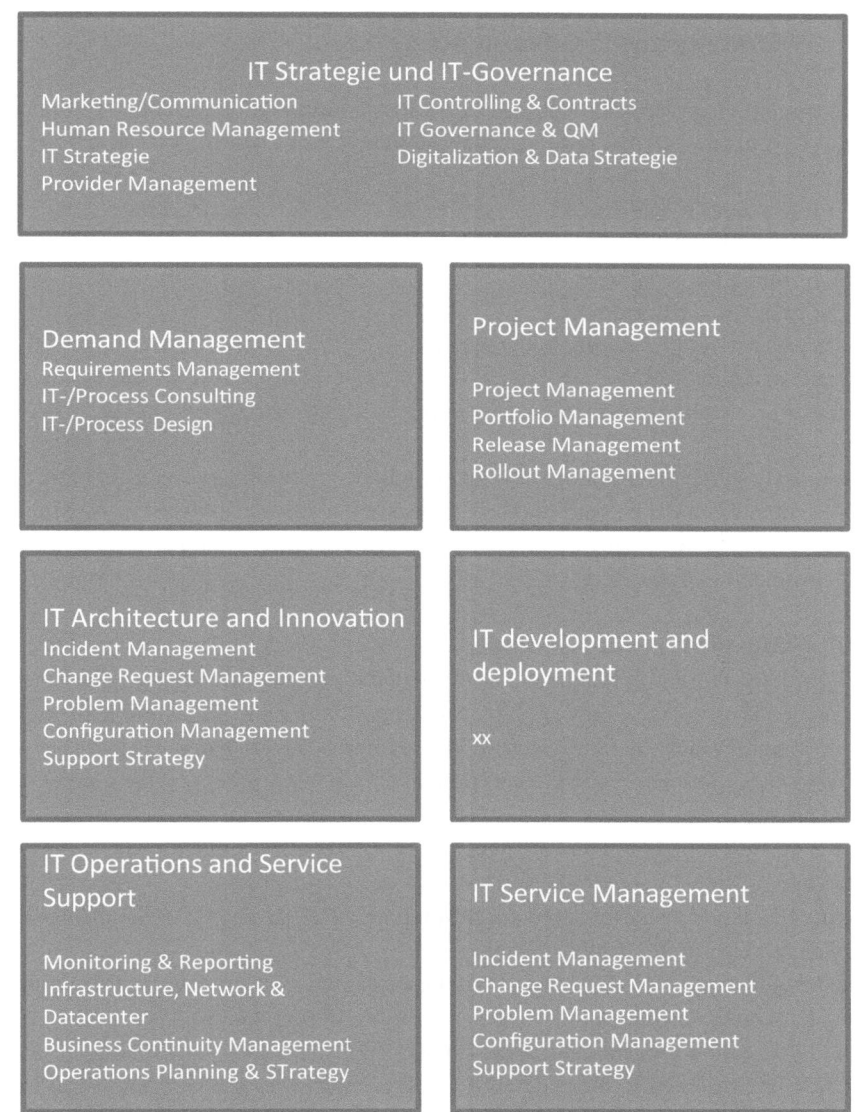

Fig. 4.4 A separate framework for the process organization of IT

The Seven Groups of IT processes at a Glance

In the following, the seven groups of IT processes from the framework in Fig. 4.4 are presented and provided with a few examples. This serves as orientation and can be used as a kind of template for your own creation of the required IT processes.

4.3.1   IT Strategy and IT Governance

IT strategy and IT governance figuratively form the umbrella of the entire IT house. The essential IT processes in this group are the following:

- IT strategy and IT roadmap.
- Marketing/communication.
- IT controlling and contracts.
- Human resource management.
- IT governance and IT quality management.
- IT purchasing and SRM.
- Provider or supplier management (including sourcing strategy).

Particularly in the environment of high compliance requirements such as FDA or GxP, increased attention must be paid to the IT processes in the environment of IT governance and quality management. However, these processes are always company-specific, so they are not presented in detail here.

4.3.1.1 IT Strategy and IT Roadmap

The IT strategy and the IT roadmap are the foundation of a functioning IT organization. Therefore, as IT processes, they are also very important for the CIO and the management to understand how such an IT strategy or IT roadmap is developed.

Two possible approaches are presented here among many others on the market, as they are very practical.

One is the development of an IT strategy in seven steps, as outlined in the author's book *IT Strategy.*

Figure 4.5 shows the seven steps for developing an IT strategy. For details on the procedure, please refer to the author's book.

The development of an IT roadmap will be explained in more detail at this point.

The IT roadmap is created in five steps, as shown in Fig. 4.6.

Step 2 ("Creating a vision and target image of IT") and step 3 ("Creating an IT roadmap") will be presented in more detail here. The other steps are well known to most IT managers or are presented elsewhere in this book (see, e.g., the IT portfolio in Sect. 4.3.3.1).

Fig. 4.5 IT strategy in seven steps

Create the Vision and Target Image of IT

In German companies, work is still very rational. Processes, structures, clear hierarchies, and work instructions still form the framework of work. Agility, network organizations, and the start-up wave are bringing movement into the tight framework from the industrial age. However, many still resist this and dismiss it as "newfangled bells and whistles."

Not everything that is new has to be good. But on the subject of vision, or today also often called purpose, a clear position should be taken here. If you have been able to experience for yourself in a few projects the power that comes from a jointly supported vision, you will experience your work as meaningful again. For years, studies have been telling us that more than half of internal employees have resigned internally. Could it be because they have lost the meaning of their work?

From there: What is the function of a vision or what is it supposed to do?

▶ **Definition** Definition of vision and objectives

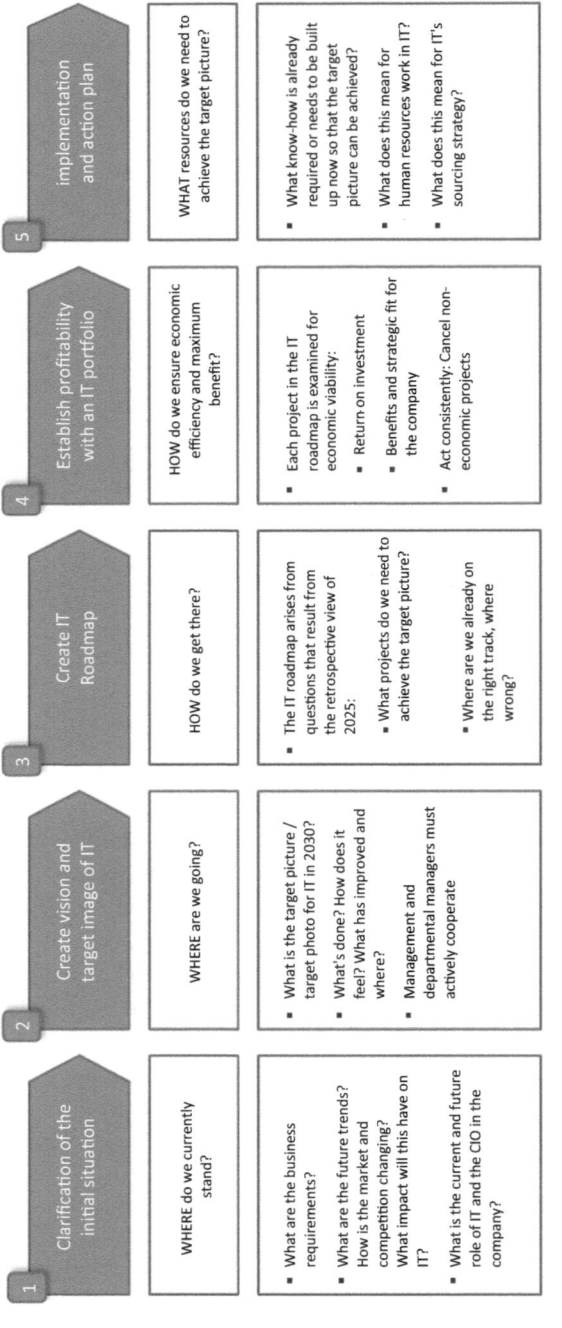

Fig. 4.6 The IT roadmap in five steps

- The vision is the foundation and basis for the strategy.
- It provides orientation for one's own actions.
- Visions are runways for goals.
- A vision that is clear and backed up with facts creates added value and benefits, and stands behind arouses conviction and, above all, provides motivation for all employees.

Admittedly: Many visions – especially those of large corporations – often come across as wooden and somehow all seem the same. How is identification supposed to take place? Why should you, as one of the thousands of employees, like it? But should you quit immediately because of it?

Corporate groups do not have it easy either. For an IT organization with between 20 and 500 employees, it is easier to formulate an IT vision that fits the entire IT and the company.

The following questions are the primary focus on the way to this vision:

- Why do we exist as IT in the company?
- What drives us?
- Where do we want to be in 3 or 5 years?

Vision is developed by going on a journey through time. This may sound strange at first, but that is what vision is all about. It is allowed to dream while working.

Which events are different from today and with which consequences can be experienced? Pictures are more important than numbers! The managers should have already been there in perspective and emotionally, where they want to get to in reality.

It has proven successful to develop the vision together with the IT management team as well as the management. This means that about five to ten people are involved. It does not have to be a joint workshop, but each participant of the group can do it for themselves at a place of their choice and when they feel like it and have time for it (you should give the participants a week for this purpose).

A neutral person can act as moderator, but the CIO can also do this himself, in which case neutrality is called into question.

The first thing to do is to set a target date. A period of at least 3–4 years and a maximum of 7–8 years in the future is suitable. Five years often forms the golden mean and so we will take January 1, 2025, as the target date.

In order to develop this vision or the so-called target image, the following questions and instructions will help:

- Each of the participants now puts himself in the year 2025.
- You look at what is happening.
- Which topics are being worked on? What are important projects?
- What are we proud of in the year 2025? What has been achieved together?
- What is all there already and what can you build on?
- How does that feel?

It is now important to write down all these findings in prose; a white sheet of paper, which you fill on a full page, is perfectly adequate. The facilitator collects these works as an objective and neutral expert for the strategy work. It is quite possible to create two or three versions of the vision or the target picture. Now each participant receives all documents with the request to evaluate them:

What is good? What is bad? What is missing?

Then comes the workshop, in which the goal is to create an overall vision or an overall goal from all the individual documents. For this purpose, all participants meet to create an overall document and an overall vision from the known individual documents. Ideally, the overall document is created "live," visible to all in a Word document, so that everyone goes home with the same result in mind.

Create the IT Roadmap

Now the path can be developed from the initial situation that exists today to the IT vision that has just emerged.

It is very important not to think from today to the IT vision in 2025, but backward.

That means specifically:

- One is transported back to the year in which one's own target image was concretized as an IT vision!
- What can be seen there? What has been achieved?
- What were the first concrete steps taken at that time?
- What measures were derived?
- What difficulties have been encountered?
- How were these mastered?
- So what does it take to even get there today?

This is the so-called work on the "strategic gap." This strategic gap refers to the area that lies between what is seen in the goal picture and what actually is today. In other words, "What is the gap between the vision and what is today?"

The IT roadmap provides an overview of all important topics, tasks, and projects for the next 2–3 years on a timeline. The general structure follows the strategy work from phase 3. The starting point of the IT roadmap is the IT assessment with its results and gaps or deltas. The goal of the IT roadmap is the IT vision, in which the gaps and deltas have been resolved as much as possible through several transformation steps. The graphic Fig. 4.7 shows an overview of the IT roadmap.

The IT roadmap thus forms a binding framework that combines the results of the IT assessment and the IT vision with the necessary transformation steps.

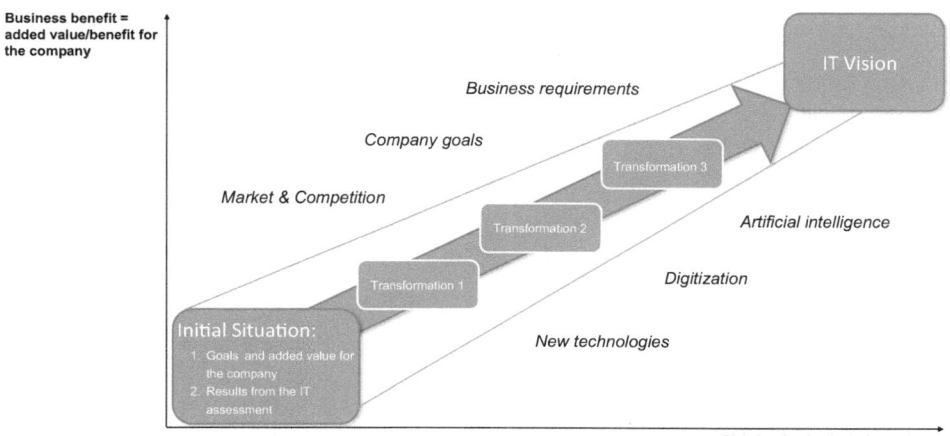

Fig. 4.7 The IT roadmap at a glance

To bring these transformation steps to life, a development plan can be placed on top of them. The steps of the transformation are then given contours and are "built on" with concrete IT projects in annual slices. Figure 4.8 shows an example of an IT roadmap with projects aligned to the target image of IT in 2025. It quickly becomes clear what will be "delivered" on the IT roadmap in the coming years and how this will contribute to the company's IT vision.

4.3.1.2 Marketing/Communication

Before strategic issues are addressed, there must be deliberate time to do so. Otherwise, the danger of an immature and, above all, unaccepted strategy and vision is very great. And quite honestly: This causes more harm than good for a CIO!

- Communication plan: Who to meet and when? Rule dates must be set for this!
- Newsletter: No prose, but three to max. Four topics and these topic sections max. 500–600 words, loosen up with professional pictures (please no screenshot collection, but pictures with the people involved), present success projects, but also openly admit the one or other negative and show how you want to get a grip on the topic (and be measured on it).

Now is the time to present this IT roadmap and ideally make it known in the company in a kind of "IT roadshow." This kills two birds with one stone:

- You create transparency and can do feedback loops with all key stakeholders to further optimize the IT roadmap.
- You set a real program for IT, which also has to be delivered. That puts you in a bind, but that is also positive, because you can be measured against it.

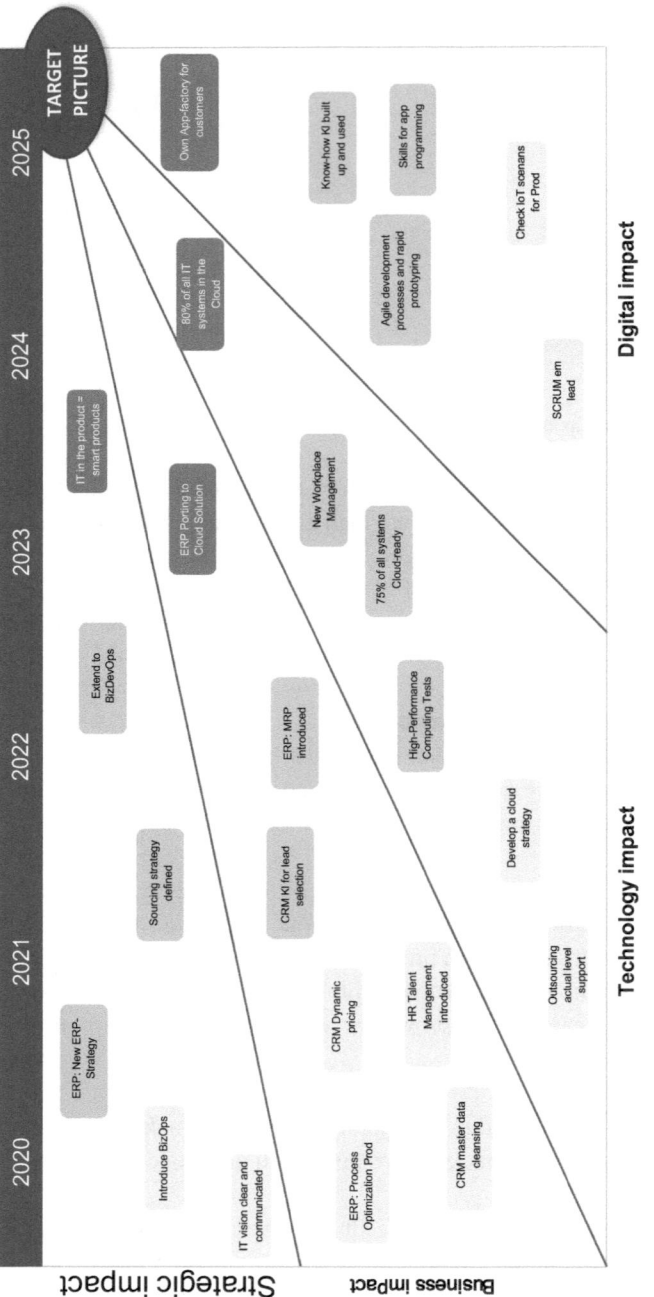

Fig. 4.8 An example of an IT roadmap with concrete projects and target image of IT in 2025

4.3.1.3 IT Controlling and Contracts

IT controlling is one of the management tools of the CIO and is also an important instrument for the management to control the IT.

Essential questions of IT can be answered – at least to some extent – by IT controlling:

- What is the value of a company's IT?
- How much should a company's IT cost?
- How could one determine the value?

IT has developed rapidly in recent years and decades. This has also been reflected in IT controlling. As seen in Fig. 4.9, in the 1990s and early 2000s, IT was seen as a cost, so at the controlling level, IT was a cost center. With the realization that IT is becoming an asset and is even seen as an equal partner, IT was no longer seen as a cost center but as a service center possibly even a profit center and was managed within the company. Through digitalization and new technologies, IT is even able to create real strategic competitive advantages in some companies. Of course, a cost center no longer makes sense, and today we speak of an "IT Strategic Investment Center."

What are the goals of IT controlling?

- IT controlling is responsible for the transparency that IT management needs in order to make the "right" decisions.
- This is done by actively accompanying and critically advising IT management in controlling control loops of IT: planning, implementation (provision and operation), variance analysis, and correction (measures).

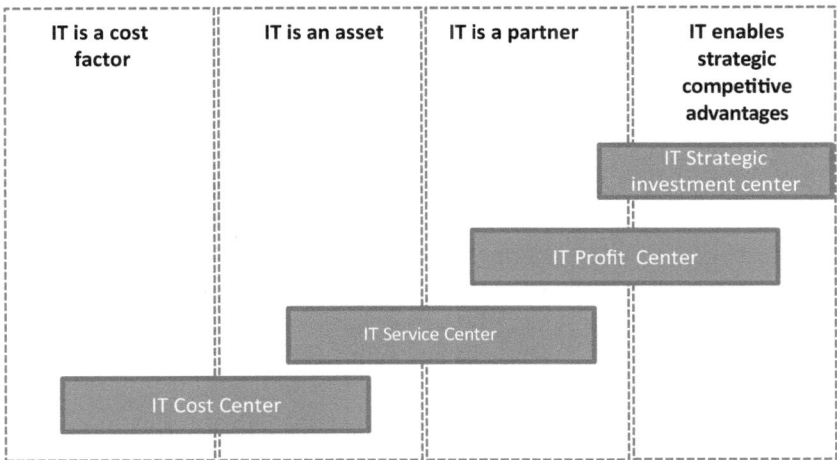

Fig. 4.9   What is the value of a company's IT?

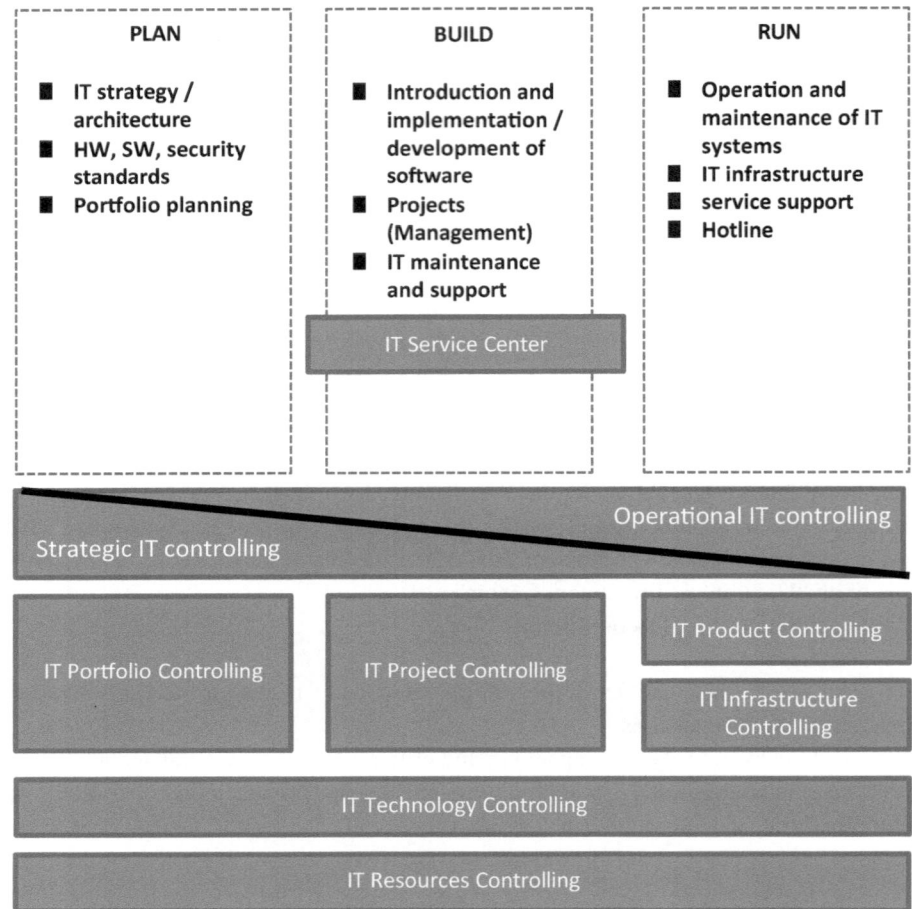

Fig. 4.10 Components of IT controlling

Following Prof. Gadatsch, Fig. 4.10 shows the components of IT controlling very clearly and differentiates between the various types of IT controlling [4].

For further discussion of the topic of IT controlling, we recommend the book *Masterkurs IT-Controlling* by Prof. Gadatsch, which is also published by Springer-Verlag.

The topic "contracts and contract management in IT" is very important for the CIO in addition to the topic "IT controlling." Reference should be made to the COBIT framework at this point. Under AI5, the topic "procurement of IT resources" is described with the subtopic AI5.2 "supplier contract management."

As an overview of the topic of "contract management," only a first outline should serve here, which shows IT-relevant components that should be contractually regulated:

- Outsourcing.
- Standard and also individual software development.
- Consulting services.
- Education and training.
- Hardware/network purchase and setup.
- Maintenance and care.

4.3.1.4 IT HR (Human Resource Management)

The personnel topics in IT are mostly the responsibility of the human resources (HR) department. Nevertheless, the topic of HR in IT is more than relevant, as IT experts are very rare on the personnel market and it is very difficult to recruit the right knowledge workers.

Therefore, in this context, we will briefly discuss the key issues of the CIO and IT leadership that are strategically important for IT.

These are the following three issues that IT leadership should focus on:

- IT personnel development and potential management.
- Training and further education for IT employees.
- IT personnel marketing.

In addition, there is another point which is described in detail in Sect. 4.3.7, namely, the job description or job role definition of all IT employees.

With regard to IT personnel development, reference can be made to a very important point in management, namely, the topic of "strengthening strengths" in Sect. 3.3.

Training and continuing education are one of the key drivers for successful IT organizations in today's world. Therefore, a detailed training and further education concept should exist in this framework, which is oriented toward the strengths of the IT experts (Sect. 3.3).

4.3.1.5 IT Purchasing and Provider or Supplier Management

The strategic and active management of IT service providers and suppliers is an important task of IT management and is unfortunately often still too much neglected.

Here, reference can again be made to COBIT on the one hand. AI5 regulates the procurement of suppliers with all its companies.

Figure 4.11 shows an overview of the definition and the four essential tasks of IT supplier management.

An important sub-item of supplier management is the sourcing strategy. Figure 4.12 shows an example of a sourcing strategy. Differentiation is made on the axes according to company criticality and internal know-how. It quickly becomes clear which services should be outsourced, checked, strengthened, or in any case left in place. This provides a very quick overview and a good and transparent communication of the supplier strategy to the management.

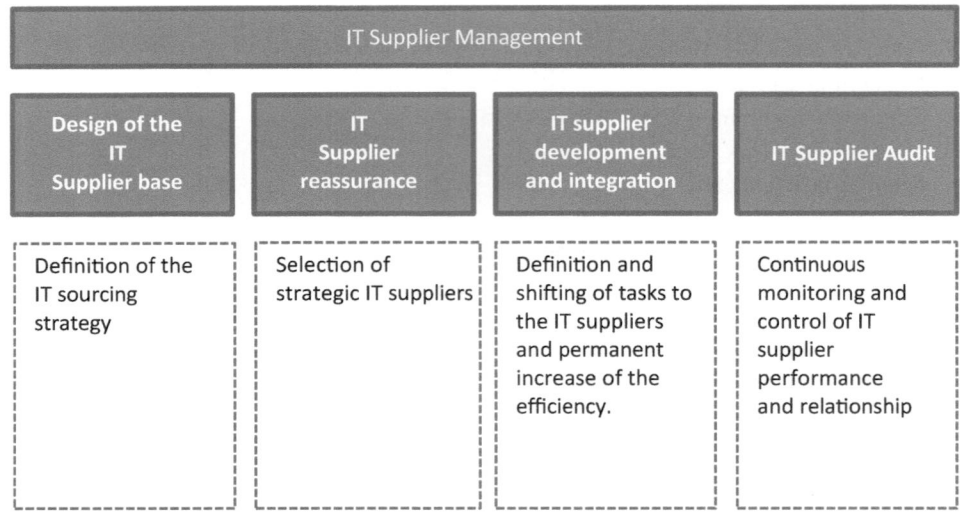

Fig. 4.11 IT supplier management at a glance

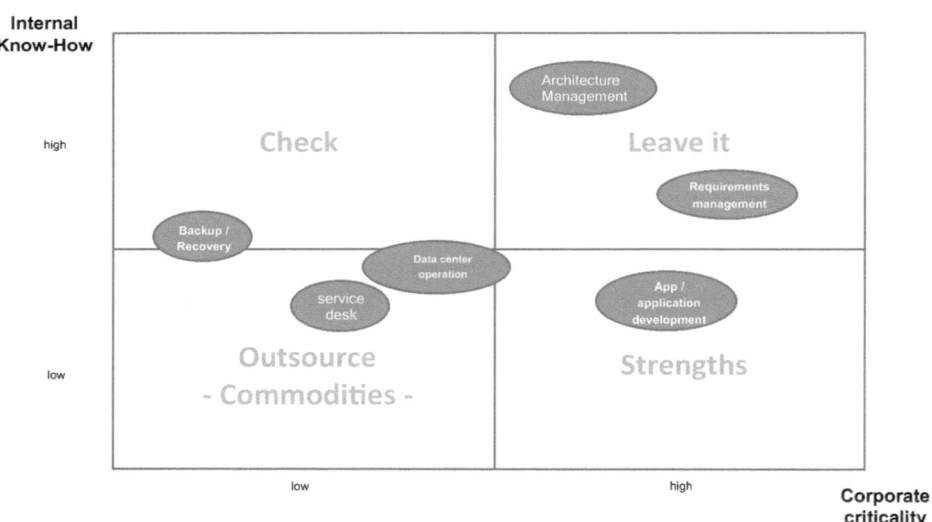

Fig. 4.12 An exemplary sourcing strategy

4.3.2   Demand Management

The following four IT processes belong to the demand management group:

- Requirements management.
- IT/process consulting.

- IT/process design.
- Demand portfolio management.

For information on IT/process consulting and design, please refer to the detailed description of the IT process organization in Sect. 3.4.5.

4.3.2.1 Requirements Management

A detailed description of an IT requirements management process can be found in COBIT under AI1 (identify automated solutions). Basically, all essential parts of requirements management are described there. Therefore, in this context, only the differences of requirements management in the classical sense versus agile approach are emphasized. This is an essential innovation since a few years that has to be taken into account.

Requirements management has become much more agile in recent years due to digitalization and increasing complexity and dynamics. Whereas the typical waterfall model used to apply to the planning of larger IT projects, the agile approach, e.g., according to SCRUM, is predominant today.

Figure 4.13 nicely shows the differences between classical requirements and project management and the agile approach. Primarily, the performance triangle is turned upside down. In the classic approach, the performance or scope of the project is clearly outlined and described in sometimes very large requirements and functional specifications in the requirements process. The time and effort, however, are correspondingly variable and difficult or impossible to plan.

In the agile context, it is exactly the opposite. Effort and time are fixed by clearly regulated sprints and recurring tests, but the scope is variable, depending on what fits into the sprint and how far you actually get in the prototype approach.

Another difference in the context of requirements management between agile and classic is that the phases of analyzing and planning are recurring in the agile context and do not take place only once as in classic planning according to the waterfall model.

Figure 4.14 shows this difference very clearly. Especially in the area of requirements management, this is a clear difference to the previous classic process model. This is because requirements management does not only take place at the beginning and during the preparation of the project, but is a recurring process that is repeated after each sprint or completed prototype. In addition to the pure methodology, this also has an impact on the role of the requirements manager. He is a permanent team member in agile teams and no longer a separate and more or less self-reliant entity.

For further details on SCRUM and agile process models, please refer to Sect. 3.3.5.

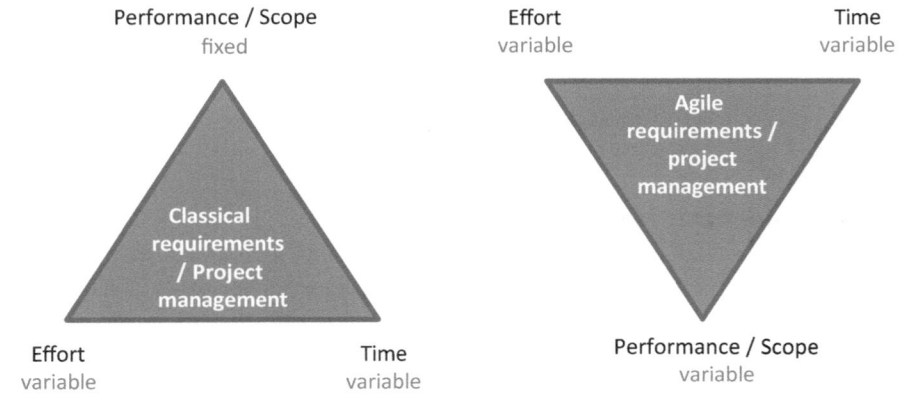

Fig. 4.13 Classic vs. agile requirements management

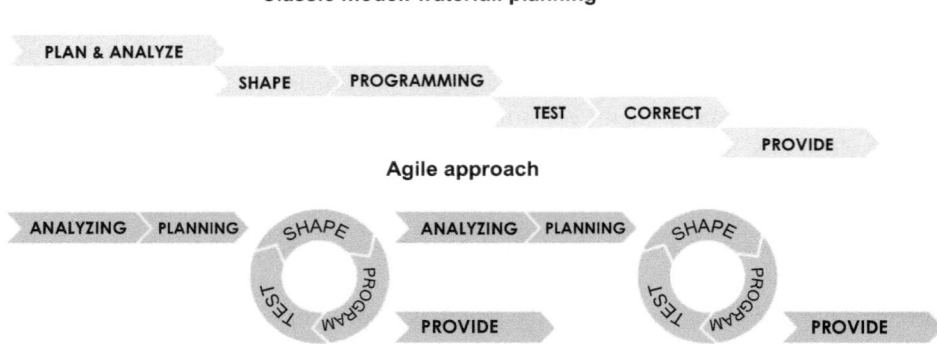

Fig. 4.14 Waterfall versus agile planning

4.3.3   Project Management

The two essential processes from the group of project management are project management itself and portfolio management. These are described and highlighted in more detail below.

Further project management processes can be seen in release and rollout management. These are precisely defined according to ITIL and therefore do not require any further definition of terms here.

4.3.3.1 Project Management

IT project management shows the classic process of how an IT project is to be planned and managed. This is explained in detail in the basic frameworks of, e.g., PRINCE2 and should not be reproduced in depth here. Nevertheless, there are a few things that need to be regulated individually for your company.

For example, it should be clear when or from which scale an IT project is talked about in your company and which classifications there are for this. Figure 4.15 provides an overview of this and can serve as a basis for the further specification for your company.

Furthermore, the subdivision of an IT project makes sense so that the complexity can be taken out and the management and control can be successful. For this purpose, for example, a breakdown into the following four project phases can be useful:

- Order clarification.
- Concept.
- Realization.
- Closing.

Figure 4.16 shows an overview of the four phases with the core questions.

A delineation of the tasks per project phase is shown in Fig. 4.17.

An overview of the documents required per project phase is equally important for IT process design. This is because clear standards can ensure professionalization and, above all, quality assurance. Figure 4.18 shows the documents that need to be prepared in each project phase.

Clarity about the roles in the project and their responsibilities is one of the key factors for a successful project. Figure 4.19 shows an overview of the project roles with their responsibilities.

In addition to the general methods and processes for the project process as described in PRINCE2 and other frameworks, the typical questions per project phase are helpful. These are shown in the following figures per project phase (Figs. 4.20, 4.21, 4.22 and 4.23).

When it comes to project management, the topic of agility in the sense of SCRUM naturally also plays a major role. Thus, the project management processes can and should

Features	Change request	Small project	Medium project	Large project
New system/technology	No	Yes	Yes	Yes
Requires a project organization	No	Yes	Yes	Yes
Internal expenditure	up to 10 PT	10 - 50 PT	50 - 250 PT	from 250 PT
Budget excl. investments	up to 10 TEUR	up to TEUR 100	up to 250 TEUR	from 250 TEUR
Approving authority	Head of SW Development	IT management circle	IT management circle	CIO
Required level for the project manager		Min. level 1	min. Level 2	Level 3
Maximum number of projects managed in parallel by one project manager		3	3	1

Fig. 4.15 Classification of IT projects

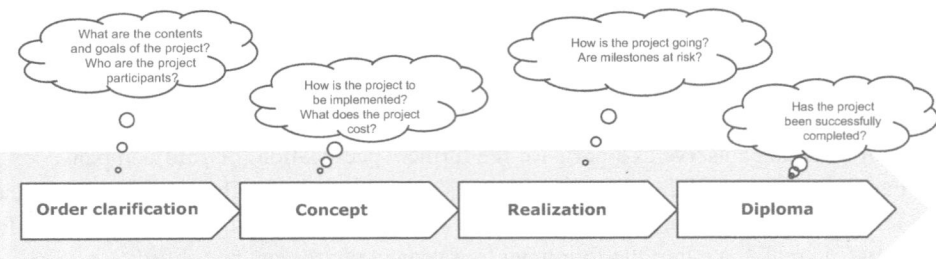

Fig. 4.16 Overview of the four project phases

also be handled according to agile methods using sprints, at least in the realization phase. See Sect. 3.4 for more information on the use of SCRUM.

4.3.3.2 Portfolio Management

In most companies, projects are part of everyday life. As a result, a veritable jumble of projects has become established – especially in IT. In order to maintain an overview, financial theory was used a few years ago, and portfolio management was taken as the basis for creating transparency in projects. Just as your financial portfolio shows you which shares, bonds, or funds you have with which development, this can also happen with projects.

Applied to the IT world, McKinsey has examined how portfolios are used in IT and to what result they contribute. The study is from 2012, but its relevance is still valid today. Here is what came out of it:

- Approximately 30% of IT projects do not serve to support the specialist departments and represent pure IT projects, the efficiency of which is often insufficiently quantifiable for the company.
- 15–20% of IT projects in a portfolio may be abandoned because they do not contribute measurably to business success.
- A further 25% of IT projects do not have to be continued in full, but also fulfill their tasks in a reduced form.
- Between 40% and 50% of all e-business initiatives do not support business objectives and do not add measurable value.

As you can see: A project portfolio can quickly help you not only get or maintain an overview but, more importantly, become more efficient. Management will thank you for this, which is why portfolio management has become one of the essential tools for CIOs, IT directors, and OIT managers.

Necessary Delimitations

Before we start, we should make a distinction for better understanding. This is because the terms project, subproject, program, and portfolio are often confused. In order to get a

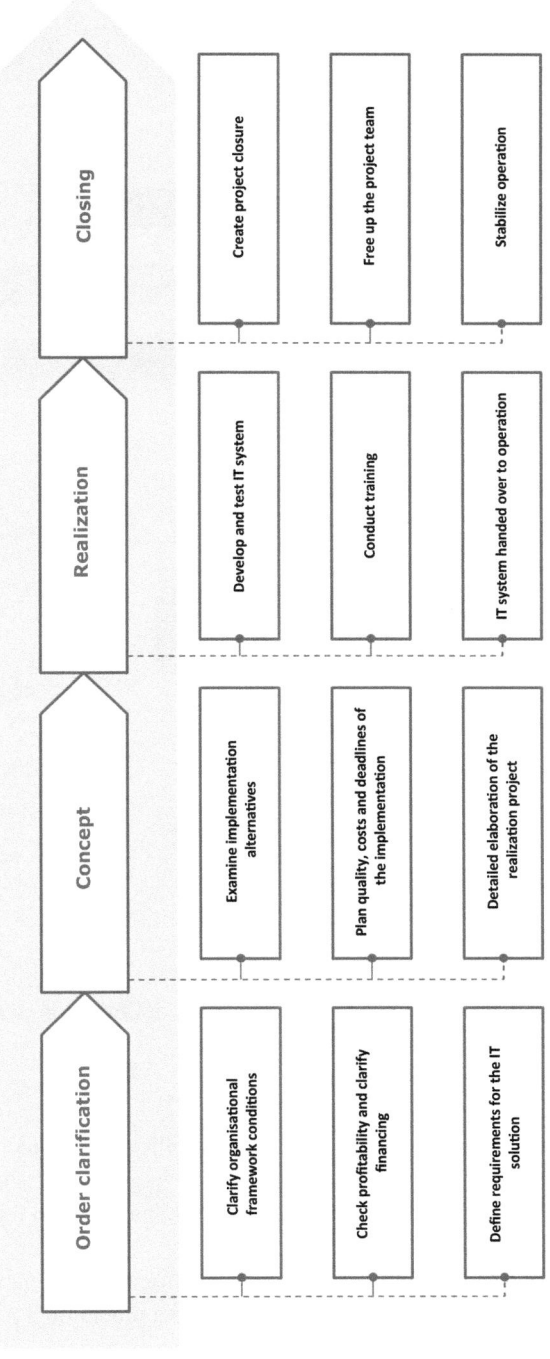

Fig. 4.17 The typical tasks in the four project phases

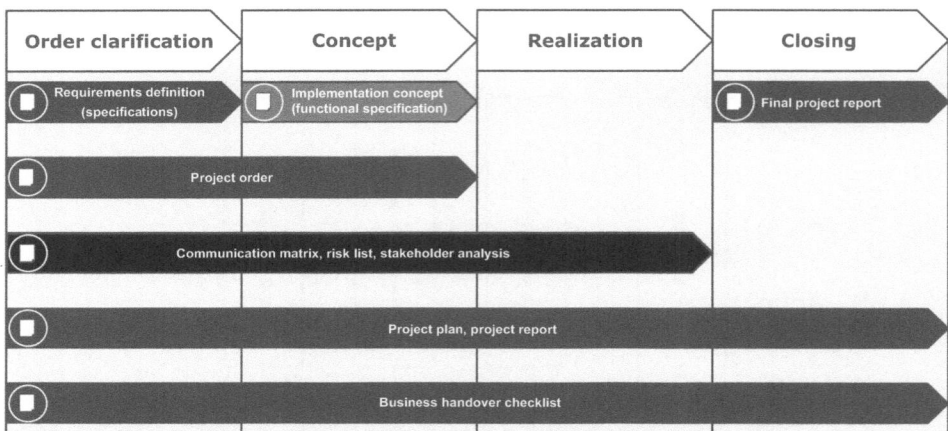

Fig. 4.18 Documents in the respective project phases

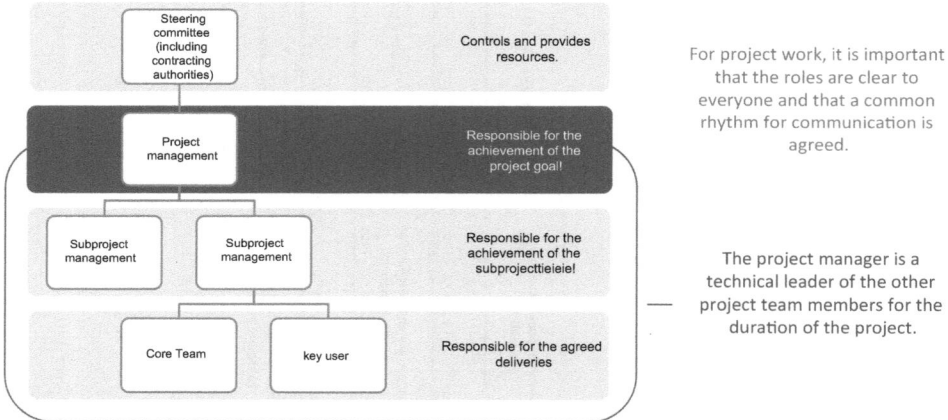

Fig. 4.19 Overview of the project roles

uniform view and to avoid confusion, the following delimitation serves as shown in Fig. 4.24.

The following things are to be distinguished:

- Projects are the smallest unit. They are the responsibility of a project manager.
- As a subunit, subprojects are occasionally created in larger projects that deal with specific topics or content. These are led by subproject managers who report to the project manager.
- A program is defined as a group of projects that fit together thematically, in terms of content, or have a common goal. The leadership is incumbent on a program manager.

„Auftragsklärung ist erst dann beendet, wenn absolute Klarheit über Zielsetzung und Rahmenbedingungen herrscht und keine Bauchschmerzen mehr existieren!"

Fig. 4.20   Questionnaire for order clarification

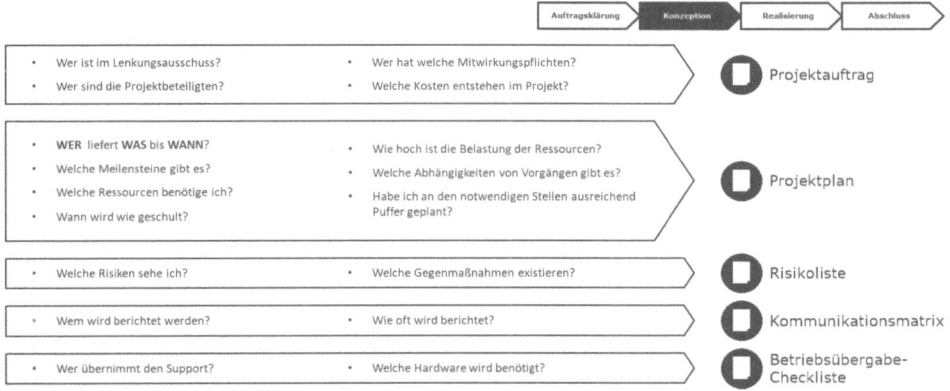

Fig. 4.21   Questionnaire for the conception

- A project portfolio is not a project or a program, but an instrument that considers all projects and programs simultaneously from the point of view of strategic prioritization. It is a permanent task in distinction to the project or program, which is always limited in time. Project portfolio management provides a cross-project overview for the analysis, control, and management of all projects and programs. Here, one has a bird's-eye view and can quickly and clearly evaluate, prioritize, and make decisions on all projects and programs. This also makes it possible to quickly identify synergies between projects. The question is: "Which are the *right* projects for our company at this point in time?" In the context of project portfolio management, strategic and financial evaluation aspects such as ROI or alignment with the UN strategy are the key benchmarks.

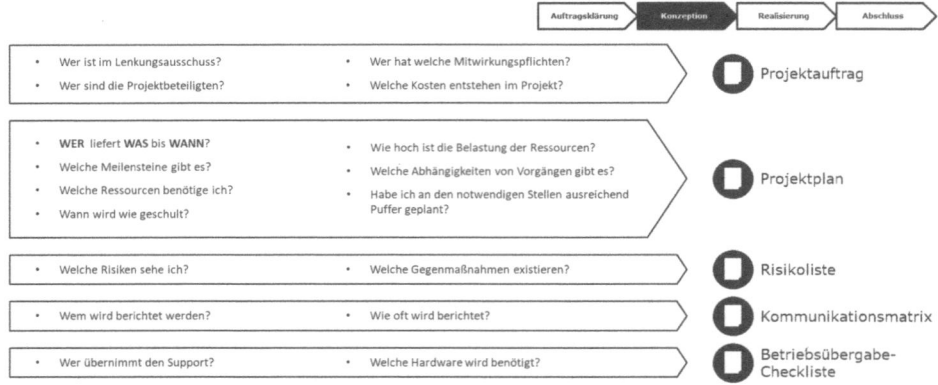

„Die Konzeptionsphase ist erst dann beendet, wenn das „Wie" für das gesamte Projekt geklärt ist und alle Ressourcen und Mitwirkungspflichten vereinbart sind."

Fig. 4.22 Questionnaire realization

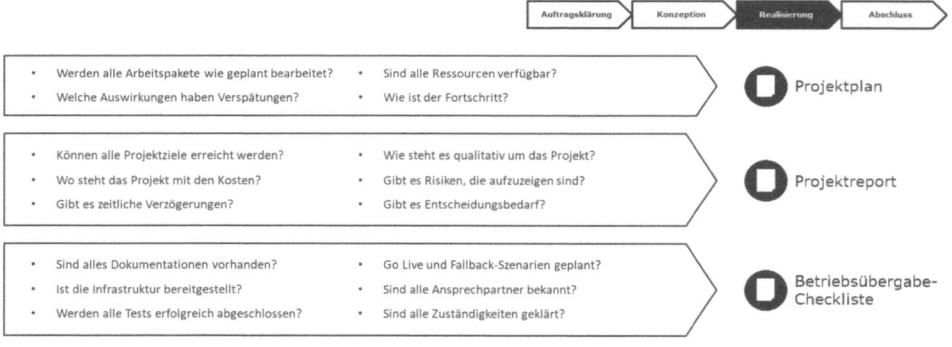

„Jede Aktion braucht Reflexion!"

Fig. 4.23 Questionnaire project closure

Therefore, project portfolio management is an ideal tool for CIOs and IT managers to strategically lead the IT organization.

There is another instrument that is often confused with the project portfolio. We are talking about multi-project management. The difference lies in the approach: Project portfolio management has a bird's-eye view of the projects and examines synergies as well as the strategically correct alignment of the projects, whereas multi-project management is characterized by a strong operational character, i.e., it acts more on the content level of the individual projects. Multi-project management describes more the operative action of leading and managing a large number of projects, whereas project portfolio management has a more strategic character in the sense of examining, assessing, and monitoring projects.

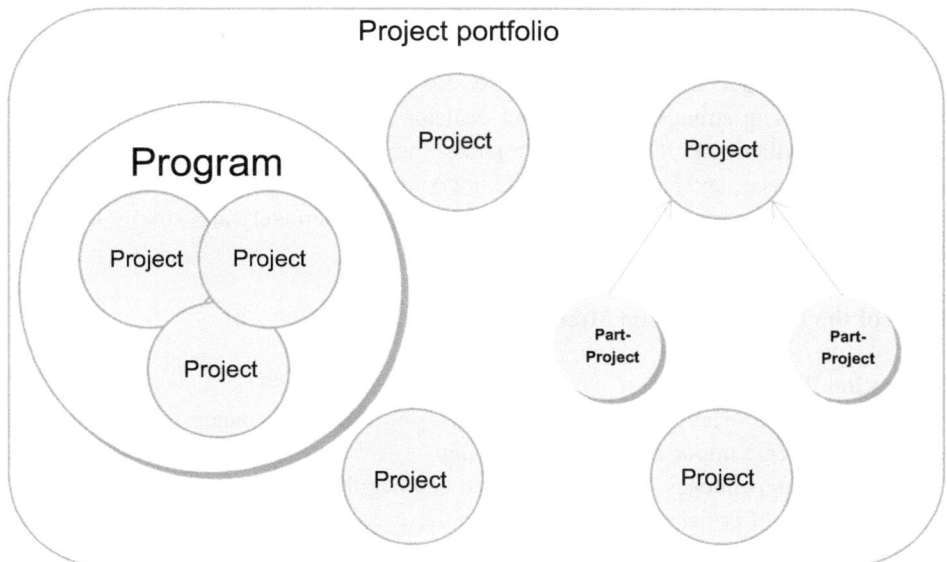

Fig. 4.24 A demarcation: projects, programs, and portfolios

Scoping: Where Does the Use of Project Portfolios Make Sense and Where Not
Project portfolios are not appropriate for all use cases. The following overview should help you assess for which use cases a project portfolio is right for you and your IT organization. These are the areas for which a project portfolio fits:

• Recognition of redundancies between projects.
• The project objectives can be better coordinated.
• Prioritization, categorization, and evaluation of new and ongoing projects and programs.
• Control and monitoring of the added value of projects and programs.
• Ideal basis for discussion for the coordination of goals with the departments.
• Basic tool for the development of an IT strategy.
• Making make-or-buy decisions.

What an IT project portfolio cannot do (out-of-scope):

• No substitute for demand and requirements management.
• It cannot replace an IT strategy.
• It does not replace the detailed tracking and monitoring within a project (project controlling) but is a strategic instrument for the selection and monitoring of all projects in the company.

Summary

With the help of professional project portfolio management, you can very quickly see where your IT budget has been optimally used for the company's purpose and where it has not. This results in strands of action and decision-making that are otherwise often not transparent. Furthermore, it is easy to recognize when IT projects no longer make strategic sense. In such cases, an IT manager should not continue to throw good money after "bad" money, but rather terminate the respective IT project immediately and simply tear down the resulting "ruin."

Tasks of the Project Portfolio Management

Evaluation Phase
- Evaluation of project applications and projects according to chances, risks, profitability, and strategic importance for the company.
- Analysis of dependencies between planned and ongoing projects.
- Prioritization of project proposals based on these assessments and analyses.
- Approval or rejection of project applications.

Progress Check
- Ongoing review of the project portfolio with regard to its alignment with corporate objectives.
- Coordination between ongoing projects in terms of resources, synergies, and conflicts.
- Monitoring of ongoing projects.

Lessons Learned
- Final evaluation of completed projects.
- Backup of empirical values from current and completed projects (this can be stored in the form of a "knowledge database" very useful for subsequent projects).

The range of tasks for project portfolio management is very wide. In many IT organizations, portfolio work begins with the collection and introduction of project ideas, continues with portfolio creation and the monitoring process, and ends with the post-calculation of completed projects. Often, however, many of the tasks mentioned are not counted as part of the portfolio process and belong more to project management. Here, however, we will include all the tasks described above in the portfolio process and describe and explain them in detail in the following Part II.

The Portfolio Process
The portfolio process consists of four main processes, each of which is assigned four sub-processes, as shown in Fig. 4.25.

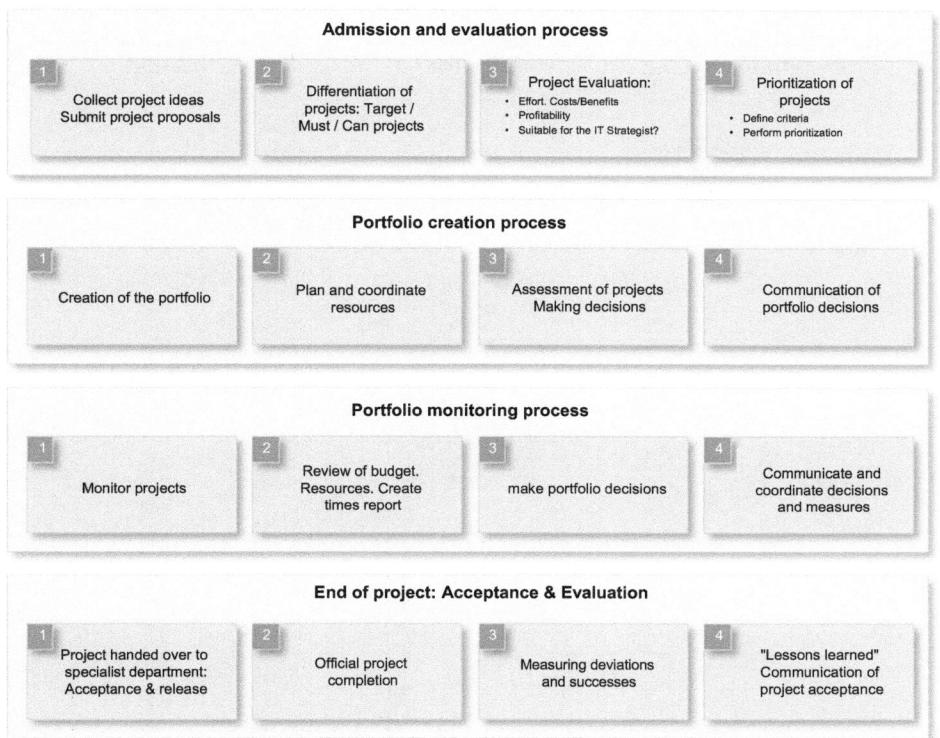

Fig. 4.25 The portfolio process

Before a detailed description of the portfolio process, it makes sense to think about the life cycle of projects as a kind of digression.

Excursus: Life Cycle of Projects
Every project is subject to a life cycle, similar to the products in the product life cycle. Before starting the portfolio process, it should be clarified in which cycle phase a project is currently located or can generally be located.

In summary, as shown in Fig. 4.26, there are the following project states:

(a) Projects before inclusion in the portfolio.
   • Project idea ("on the horizon").
   • Project applied for.
   • Deferred project.
(b) Projects in the portfolio monitoring process.
   • Approved project.
   • Ongoing project.
   • Interrupted project.

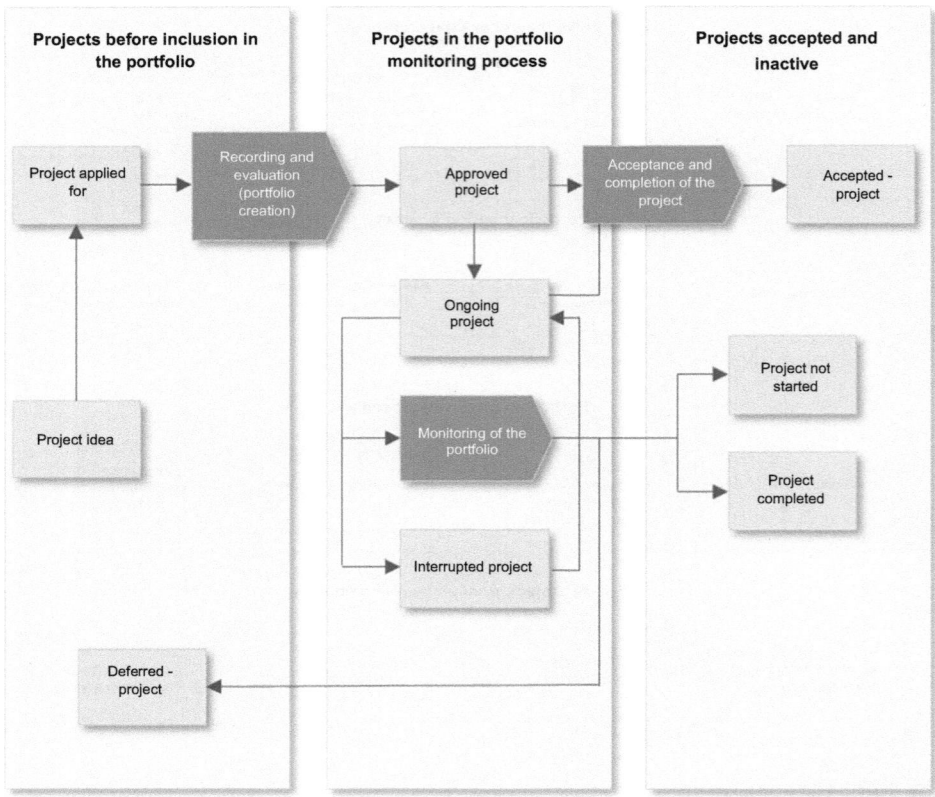

Fig. 4.26 The life cycle of projects

(c) Projects accepted and inactive.
- Projects accepted.
- Projects not started.
- Cancelled projects.

Phase 1: The Recording and Evaluation Process
The first main process begins with the acceptance of projects in the form of project ideas, which then lead to a project application, provided that the project is considered to have a certain probability of realization. In the project application, some information about the project is summarized in a structured way for the first time, such as:

- Project name.
- Project number (if available).
- Department or division responsible for the project.

- Cost center (internal transfer of project costs).
- Project objective.
- Project focus: in-scope and out-of-scope.
- Possible project start.
- Approximate project duration.
- Project risks.

All projects that are officially applied for must then be evaluated and prioritized by a committee responsible for the portfolio process and thus filtered to some extent according to certain criteria.

It is important to differentiate between project evaluation and project prioritization. Project evaluation serves to determine whether a project will be implemented or not. The prioritization of a project serves to develop an implementation sequence and thus only applies to the projects that did not fall through the filter in the evaluation as a mandatory project.

The criteria for evaluating projects must be defined individually and relate to monetary factors, risk factors, and profitability or cost/benefit factors. In prioritization, the criteria are often more difficult to grasp, and in many companies, this evaluation is subject to subjective decisions by the committee leaders. In the upcoming phase 2 (portfolio creation process), the project portfolio is created or updated for the first time, and three possible views are presented to assess the prioritization of the projects.

Phase 2: The Portfolio Creation Process
After the projects have been roughly pre-filtered in the first phase, these projects are now brought into the portfolio. In this phase, either an existing project portfolio is brought up to date or a project portfolio is created for the first time.

First, in addition to the project data collected in phase 1, the following information in particular must be determined:

- Profitability of the project in the form of a ROI (return on investment).
- The risk of the project (usually a rather subjective parameter instead of a mathematically derivable one).

In order to prioritize the projects according to the criteria just described, there are different views of the portfolio:

The axis values used for the IT portfolio are, on the ordinate, the "return on investment (ROI)" as a quantitative value of the respective project or expressed qualitatively if the ROI is difficult to determine: the benefit of the project for the company. On the abscissa, the values used can vary in order to obtain different statements about the projects. Possible statements can be:

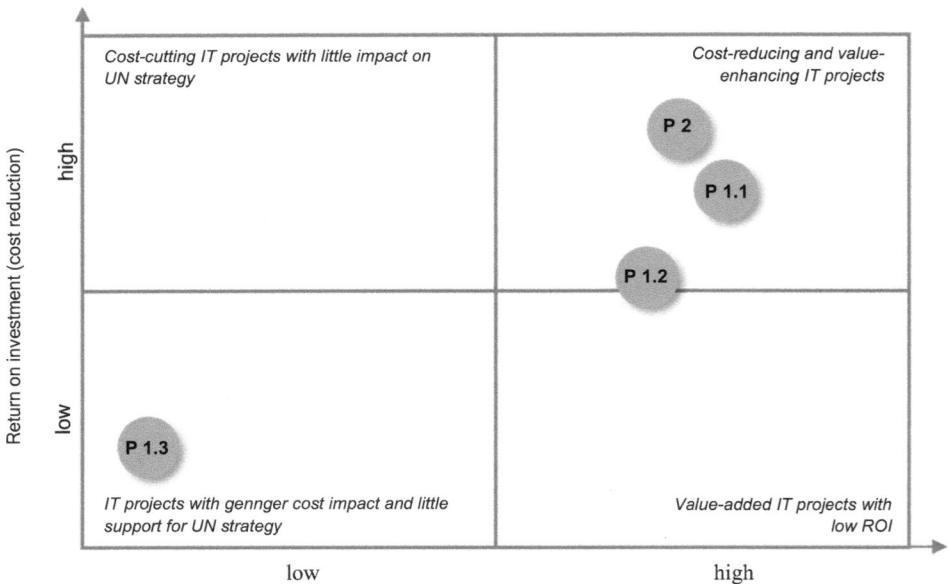

Return on investment (cost reduction)

Cost-cutting IT projects with little impact on UN strategy

Cost-reducing and value-enhancing IT projects

P 2

P 1.1

P 1.2

P 1.3

IT projects with gennger cost impact and little support for UN strategy

Value-added IT projects with low ROI

high

low

low   high

Contribution to supporting the corporate strategy (value enhancement)

Fig. 4.27   The benefit- and strategy-oriented IT portfolio

- Contribution to the support of the corporate strategy (the so-called benefit- and strategy-oriented IT portfolio).
- Realization risk or "benefit- and risk-oriented portfolio".

The Benefit- and Strategy-Oriented IT Portfolio

The benefit- and strategy-oriented IT portfolio assesses the extent to which the project serves the corporate strategy (see Fig. 4.27).

It can be clearly seen in the figure that all four sample projects (P1.1, P1.2, P1.3, and P2) have taken a different place in the portfolio. For example, subproject P1.1 is a "SAP implementation project in foreign locations" and has been classified in the upper right quadrant as a "cost-reducing and value-enhancing project." In contrast to P2 (DMS implementation), which was also shown in this quadrant, the benefit for the company or the ROI for P1.1 is not as high as for the DMS implementation. This classification can be based on clear calculations, but in the case of the introduction of portfolio management, this can also be based on subjective opinions of the boards, which of course have to be recorded for argumentation. In this case, it is the case that the portfolio committee (more on the composition of such a committee in the section "organizational integration" at the end of the document) has decided that the DMS introduction has a greater benefit than the SAP introduction in the foreign locations, since currently all documents are filed manually in folders and the bookings are available in SAP, but still have to be stored physically.

This can be automated, and thus jobs can be saved, and a much more efficient structure for searching and finding documents is made possible. Subproject P1.3 (introduction of SAP FI/CO) goes hand in hand with the two subprojects P1.1 and P1.2 and is also just about classified in the upper right quadrant. However, the value added and cost savings here are not quite as high as in the related subprojects, since the current expenses are not directly reduced by the introduction of SAP FI/CO and thus no direct ROI will be immediately apparent. However, due to the interdependence of the three subprojects, it must be said that they support each other and are therefore not classified far apart in the portfolio. Project P2 (introduction of SEPA) has been sorted into the lower right quadrant as it offers no strategic benefit to the business as the previous settlement worked just as well and also offers no benefit on the cost or return side, only costing money. It is to be carried out as a legal requirement but basically just adds effort that does not deliver any strategic benefit. Projects that end up in this quadrant should be terminated as soon as possible after reconsideration, as they deliver no benefit and only generate costs. In such cases, a portfolio is very helpful because it very quickly shows visually which projects deliver real benefits and which projects can be terminated quickly because they only produce costs but deliver no benefits.

The Benefit- and Risk-Oriented IT Portfolio
Frequently, the risk of IT projects is considered in the respective project, but often not in the overall context of all ongoing projects. Unfortunately, this often leads to a high rate of failed IT projects. Therefore, a risk assessment of all projects is recommended. In our example, the ROI is again shown on the ordinate, and the risk of the project is shown on the abscissa in the following figure – in accordance with the benefit- and strategy-oriented portfolio.

It quickly becomes visually clear in this portfolio that all projects definitely contain a risk that is greater than 30%. Therefore, a detailed risk and quality management must be introduced for all projects in order to keep the risks under control (Fig. 4.28).

However, only one project with a risk of failure greater than 50% is to be found in the portfolio: the introduction of SAP in the foreign locations. What is important in the classification and evaluation is the type of risk underlying the project. Here it is not so much the actual technical implementation of SAP in the foreign locations, but the training and subsequent use of SAP. The problem is the low level of qualification in the foreign locations in the specialist departments that then have to work with SAP. The best SAP installation is useless if the operation and functions are not used properly. Therefore, close and direct cooperation with the affected departments at the headquarters as well as in the foreign locations is particularly advisable in order to make the project a success.

Phase 3: The Portfolio Monitoring Process
After the project portfolio has been created or updated, the next step is to analyze and monitor the projects. The following tasks are part of the monitoring of the projects:

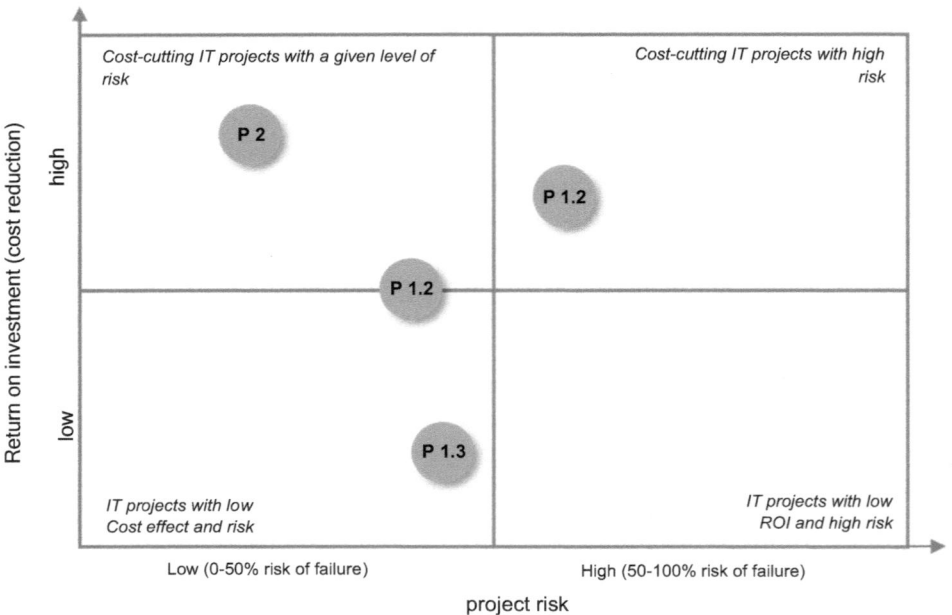

Fig. 4.28 The benefit- and risk-oriented IT portfolio

- Review of projects according to the usual project triangle factors of time, cost, and quality.
- Review and classification of the projects according to the three portfolio levels presented in phase 2.
- Contribution to the support of the corporate strategy.
- Realization risk.
- Probability of realization.
- Making decisions about reclassifying or continuing or stopping projects in the project portfolio (see the following graphic Fig. 4.29 as a decision matrix).

Once the decisions have been made, they must be communicated, along with the measures derived from them, to all those affected (it is important here to involve all those affected in the department if they were not involved in the decision).

Phase 4: End of Project – Acceptance and Evaluation
The final phase of the project portfolio process is about project closure. Here again, four sub-steps are considered:

- The official handover of the project to the faculty.
- The official project completion: The project must be finally evaluated and accepted by the business department; only then can the project be considered officially completed

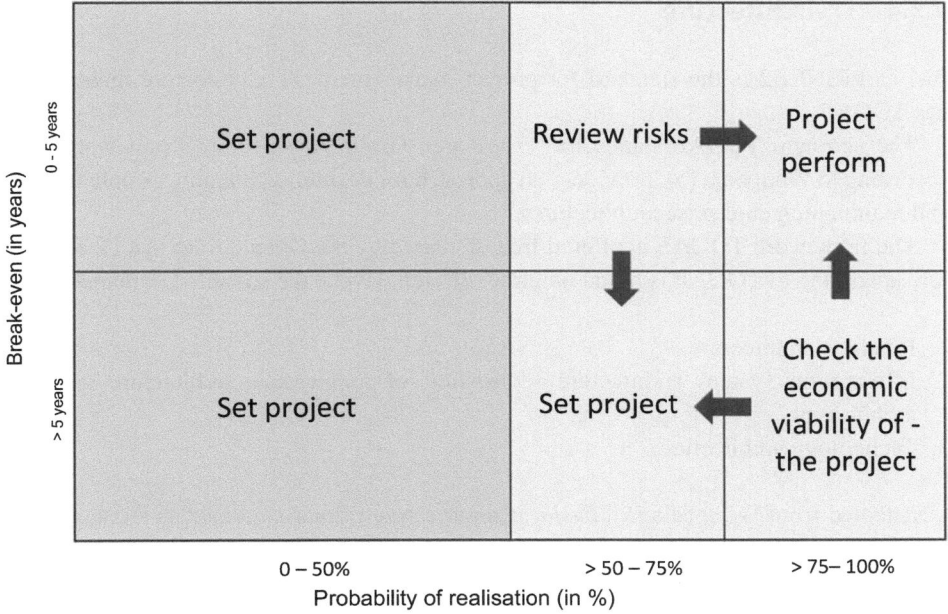

Fig. 4.29 Project decisions

in IT, and it passes over to operations, which regulates the further support of the underlying application through a maintenance contract.

- Measure deviations and achievements: After the official closure, outstanding deviations must be recorded.
- Lessons learned: In a workshop round characterized by openness, important findings are discussed, and measures for follow-up projects are derived from them.

This completes the process of portfolio assessment of IT projects.

Organizational Integration
Responsibility for the project portfolio management process should report directly to the CIO or IT manager and function as a staff unit. Only through direct connection to the CIO can efficiency be ensured and political trench warfare can be proactively excluded.

In addition to direct CIO responsibility, the close involvement of the specialist departments is critical to success. This is done through a board or committee that must meet regularly.

It is important that the decisions made by the portfolio committee are communicated and transparent. Every employee must know which projects have been prioritized and for what reason. This is the daily work and motivation basis in the project business of an IT organization.

4.3.4   IT Architecture

Just as PRINCE2 is the standard for project management, IT architecture management has TOGAF.

The acronym TOGAF stands for "The Open Group Architecture Framework" and, according to Wikipedia [5], provides "an approach for designing, planning, implementing, and maintaining enterprise architectures."

The framework TOGAF is offered free of charge by the Open Group. An IT architecture according to TOGAF is based on three different levels, the so-called domains:

1. Business architecture.
2. Information system architecture (consisting of application architecture and data architecture).
3. Technology architecture.

Adapted from Wikipedia [5], *business architecture* primarily considers strategy, organizational structure, business processes, and business capabilities.

The *information system architecture* consists of the data architecture, in which the data with its relationships that are required for the execution of the business processes are identified and described. In addition, the information system architecture includes the application architecture, which manages the applications required to execute the business processes. In addition to the inventory management of all applications, the relationships and interfaces between the applications are also considered in the context of the application architecture. The applications are categorized based on their business functionality and the information they process.

Finally, the **technology architecture** describes the architectural elements for building and operating the IT infrastructure. It defines the basis on which applications can be procured, integrated, and operated.

These base architectures can be supplemented by further architectures, depending on the perspective, for example, the security architecture (description of the security processes, the security systems, and the tasks of the organizational units involved with which the information security suitable for the organization is achieved) and the operational architecture (operation and management of the software, hardware, and communication infrastructure).

At this point, the roughly outlined TOGAF framework is recommended for working on the IT architecture. Further information can be found free of charge at https://www.opengroup.org/togaf (version 9.2 can currently be downloaded there).

4.3.5   IT Development and Deployment

Various process models can be distinguished in software development. Figure 4.30 shows eight different ways of developing software and differentiates according to the degree of formalization in the procedure model and the speed.

It can be seen that the agile and prototype-based process models are clearly superior in speed to the classic models such as the waterfall and V models. In terms of the degree of formalization, the new software development models are also significantly more informal and easier to handle.

Nevertheless, depending on the requirements situation and complexity, it makes sense to look closely at which of these process models has the greatest probability of success.

SCRUM and KANBAN have been presented in detail in this book in the context of modern forms of organization (see Sects. 3.4 and 3.4.1.2). A great deal of information on the other process models is available free of charge on the Internet, so that a detailed description is not provided here.

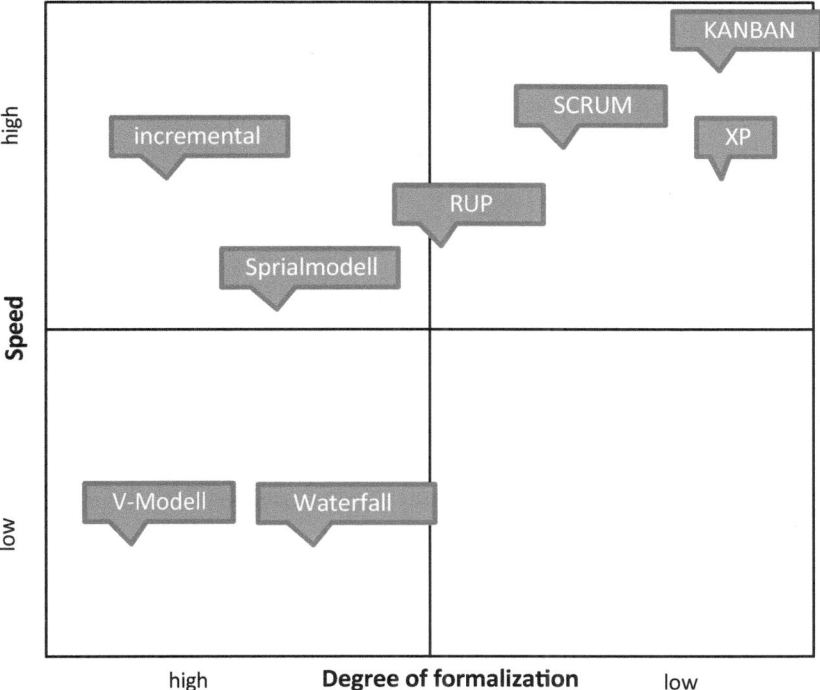

Fig. 4.30 Software development process models

4.3.6   IT Service Management

When it comes to IT service management, ITIL has been the sole standard for many years. Section 4.2.1.2 has already dealt with ITIL. Therefore, not all ITIL processes are presented here when it comes to the individual consideration of the company's own IT processes, but rather the five essential ITIL processes from the author's point of view are explained very briefly. Based on experience, these are the main drivers for more efficiency in IT service management, at least for medium-sized companies:

- Support strategy.
- Incident management.
- Problem management.
- Change request management.
- Configuration management.

In this context, the topic of IT helpdesk can serve as an example. This is often still regulated in such a way that every IT employee answers the phone and takes care of malfunctions or problems. This has grown historically in most companies but leads to the fact that many IT employees are constantly pulled out of their work. As knowledge workers, IT experts in particular need peace and quiet in order to be able to concentrate on their work, or they need to work in teams to drive projects forward.

A solution to this problem can be found, for example, through clear service definitions, as found in ITIL in the support strategy. With this, efficiency gains can be realized very quickly, such as:

- A "first-time-solution-rate" of, e.g., 60–70%, i.e., 60–70% of all incoming fault calls can be solved immediately.
- The "shift problem" and the "semi-legal" readiness of IT employees at night and on weekends would be legalized.
- Increase in customer satisfaction.
- Every problem/fault is documented and is transparent and traceable for everyone (IT and specialist department).
- Reports and statistics are possible, for better management and control of the service desk.
- Clearly defined SLAs (service-level agreements), with the possibility of penalties for non-compliance.

In addition, the definition and listing of all IT services required in the company, their associated IT systems, and system managers are a very useful task in this context.

It is also helpful if each IT service is assigned to a maintenance type, i.e., how often and when is such an IT service maintained and serviced. This should be done on the basis of the criticality of the business process underlying the IT service.

4.3.7   IT Operations

In addition to pure IT service management, IT operations deals with the provision and maintenance of hardware and software. This also includes the following processes, which are not presented here in their entirety, but as exemplary IT processes:

- Operations planning and strategy.
- Monitoring and reporting.
- Infrastructure, network, and data center.
- Business continuity management/emergency planning.

4.4   IT Personnel and Roles: Defining the Right Roles for the IT Processes

4.4.1   The CIO's First Reporting Level

A detailed description of the CIO's role is given in a separate chapter of this book (Sect. 3.4.4). This chapter deals with the first reporting level of the CIO.

Classically, the CIO has three or four direct reports, which are generally set up either according to plan, build, or run and classically according to application development, operations, and infrastructure and possibly processes/organization or project management. This is still common in many mid-sized companies today. Figure 4.31 shows an example of this.

In addition, there are assistant functions and staff functions for controlling, finance, legal, purchasing, and strategy and governance. Depending on the size of the company, these can be combined into one person or role, or in the case of large groups, there is one role or even more for each of these.

In today's times of digital transformation, two roles have also proven to be very important for the CIO. One is the IT chief architect (see the role description in Fig. 4.32), as the system landscape has become increasingly complex over the years. The second is the CISO (see the role description in Fig. 4.33), the chief information security officer, who is responsible for IT and cybersecurity. This is also an increasingly important field in a modern IT organization.

4.4.2   IT Strategy and IT Governance

The typical staff functions of the CIO are grouped in the IT strategy and governance area.

Figure 4.34 shows the role of the IT controller.

Another important role in this cluster is that of the officer for IT governance and, in this example, also for IT purchasing (see Fig. 4.35). The purchase of IT services as well as

Executive PLAN / BUILD / RUN

Job Objectives:

- Disciplinary and technical management of employees

- Strategic orientation, organization and management of the department

Tasks

- Leading the employees in the IT area

- Responsibility for personnel, budget and results

- Evaluation of new technologies and their use for continuous optimization

- Contact person and coordinator for external IT service providers

- PLAN: Responsible for requirements and portfolio management as well as first point of contact for all departments.

- BUILD: Responsible for the definition and maintenance of software development processes

- RUN: Responsible for the operation and security of the entire IT operations / Responsible for the smooth IT service management

Fig. 4.31 Executive direct report to the CIO

hardware and software can of course also be carried out by the company's central purchasing department, but here a role has been deliberately created that explicitly deals with this within IT but of course adheres to the technical specifications of central purchasing.

Other roles are also conceivable in large companies, such as:

- Speakers for IT strategist.
- Provider manager.
- Organization and transformation manager.
- Asset and license manager.
- Quality manager.
- HR and skills manager.

4.4.3 Demand Management

In the demand or requirements management cluster, the focus is on the requirements manager as outlined as an example role in Fig. 4.36.

IT Chief Architect

Job Objectives:

- Establish scalable and future-proof IT architecture for the company

- Customer-oriented and agile action within the framework of a
  strategic development plan

Tasks

- Management of the IT architecture team

- Research on new technologies and products

- Documentation of the actual and target IT system landscape

- Technical management of the solution architects

- Responsibility for the technical design of IT solutions

Headcount: 1 FTE

Fig. 4.32 The IT chief architect

The requirements manager has many different designations. Thus, one often encounters the in-house consultant, the process consultant, the design expert, the requirements engineer, and probably many other terms. The task of requirements management, the conception, the profitability analysis, and the interface between IT and business departments is the same or similar for all of them.

An example of an in-house consultant compared to a requirements manager is shown in Fig. 4.37.

In some companies, you will also find the so-called business relationship manager (BRM) and in a management function the so-called DIO (divisional information officer), based on the CIO, who is responsible below the CIO for a certain division or business unit.

The solution architect should also be included in this cluster. This is because he or she also forms the link between demand and supply and can completely overview and evaluate the functional requirements from the functional description to the implementation and finally decide which software should ideally be used for which requirements.

CISO - Chief Information Security Officer

Job Objectives:

- Forward-looking IT security management with a view to achieving the optimum benefit

- Achieving contractual service agreements with IT contractors

Tasks

- You establish an information security management system (ISMS), define protection goals and create information security specifications.

- You are responsible for the information security process

- They assess threats, conduct protection needs and comprehensive risk analyses, initiate necessary information security measures and verify their effectiveness.

- You are the central contact person for reports and questions on the subject of

- They manage information security incidents, vulnerabilities and threats and develop appropriate and workable solutions.

- They initiate and coordinate awareness-raising and training measures. You report regularly to the Management Board and advise it on information security matters and report to the information security team on status, risks and security incidents.

Fig. 4.33 CISO – chief information security officer

4.4.4   Project Management

In the foreground, of course, is the project manager, as exemplified in Fig. 4.38.

Here, too, PRINCE2 or the Society for Project Management in Germany offers numerous certifications with a wide range of qualifications and, accordingly, of course, different role models.

In addition to the project manager, the portfolio manager plays an important role in the strategic management of all projects (Fig. 4.39).

IT controlling and law

Job Objectives:

- Forward-looking cost management, taking into account the achievement of the optimum benefit

- Achieving contractual performance agreements with IT contractors

Tasks

- Cost management with cost elements, cost centers and cost objects

- Participation regarding the economic efficiency/TCO determination of IT strategies

- Allocation of costs to IT customers based on causation

- Forecast of investment and operating costs, verification of cost drivers

- Development and tracking of key performance indicators for IT systems and processes

- Establishment of a license management

- Preparation and coordination of IT contracts (projects, non-disclosure agreements, management/SLAs)

- Participation in data protection issues

Headcount: 1 FTE

Fig. 4.34 IT controller

Project assistance as PMO (project management office) is also important here and is described in Fig. 4.40.

In addition, there are roles such as the project controller or the project coach or facilitator.

4.4.5   IT Architecture, Innovation, and Digitalization

On the architecture level, two different roles can be differentiated:

- The enterprise architect.

IT Purchasing / IT Governance

Job Objectives:

- Coordination of IT procurement and interface to central purchasing department

- Marketing measures for corporate IT to create transparency about IT projects and tasks and as a communication channel to users

- Ensuring and maintaining all relevant IT documentation

Tasks

- IT Purchasing: Coordination of all procurement processes in IT, accompanying project-related tenders, checking incoming deliveries for IT, invoice checking with IT controlling, interface to the Central Purchasing Department

- Administration of the IT area in the in-house intranet

- Preparation, writing, interviewing, proofreading and sending of the IT newsletter

- Maintain and create the necessary governance documents (e.g. Book of Standards)

Headcount: 1 FTE

Fig. 4.35 IT purchasing/IT governance

- The application architect.

The enterprise architect is responsible for decisions about the entire IT system landscape. This includes, for example, decisions on architecture frameworks, the way architecture is operated (e.g., service-oriented), but also on development environments and above all on all systems of the IT map, and he maintains the development plan across systems.

The application architect (also called system architect) is responsible for architectural decisions for a very specific application or IT system (e.g., SAP). At this level, he is also responsible for the application architecture, for example, for all subsystems of the SAP system as well as their interfaces and data management.

Requirements Manager
(Example end-to-end process: plan-to-ship or production / logistics)

Job Objectives:

- Recording, processing, evaluating and communicating IT requirements from the fields of logistics, production

- Process management for the department of production and logistics

- Project management of selected topics

Tasks

- Development of the process strategy and the business process map

- Management of projects for the introduction, adaptation or replacement of systems to support logistics and production processes

- Requirements management in the sense of recording change requirements in Prod/Logistics, prioritization, resource planning as well as communication and coordination with the departments Prod/Log and IT/BUILD

- Planning and modeling processes

- Simulation and cost as well as key figure planning and tracking of processes in the field of Prod/Log (process controlling), incl. potential analyses of processes

- Presence in the committees of the process owners for Prod/Log

Headcount: 1 FTE

Fig. 4.36 Requirements manager

Furthermore, there are many other roles that are similar in nature, for example, the solutions architect. This person is often responsible for a specific business solution across several software systems.

In the field of digitalization and new technologies, a lot of new job profiles and roles are opening up. These may include, for example, the Big Data expert or business/data scientist or an IoT/KI expert.

Especially in the SCRUM environment, there are the following roles, which will not be described further here, but which can serve as an introduction and further research if required:

Fig. 4.37 In-house consultant

- Product owner.
- Scrum master.
- Developer.
- DevOps.
- Software architects.
- UX designer/usability experts.
- Field experts.
- Chief product owner.
- Agile coach.

4.4.6   IT Development/Deployment

In the area of IT development and provision, three roles can be roughly differentiated:

IT Project Manager

Job Objectives:

- Management of projects for the introduction, adaptation or replacement of IT systems with the following core tasks:

Tasks

- Project definition: Setting up IT projects with the topics goal, clarifying the task, budget, time frame, conception of the requirements

- Implementation of project planning (setting of milestones and activities, effort estimation)

- Define IT project organization in terms of roles involved in the project, governance (e.g. steering committee), communication behavior and rules of cooperation

- Leading and controlling IT projects: Technical leadership of the project staff

- Project controlling/status check (determination of actual/target deviations in the project and information on the status of the project)

- Escalation of conflict situations when deadlines or costs are not met

- Adherence to the scheduled and economic project goals according to the project order within the given framework conditions

- Timely information of the project committee in case of endangerment of the project deadlines and proposal of suitable measures for countermeasures

Fig. 4.38 Project manager

- Application designer.
- Application developer.
- Test specialist.

4.4.7   IT Service Management

Service management in IT is characterized by the ITIL roles. These are very clearly presented on the basis of the IT process map by Andrea and Stefan Kempter and comprise a total of 34 roles [6], which are also shown in Fig. 4.41.

Portfolio Manager

Job Objectives:

- Strategic monitoring and tracking of the IT portfolio

- Contact person for all departments with regard to the overall view of all IT projects (advisory and methodical)

Tasks

- Development of the IT portfolio process as well as collaboration in the operationalization of the portfolio strategy

- Agreement on and application of selection criteria for the inclusion and exclusion of projects from the joint cross-divisional project portfolio.

- The compilation, prioritisation and management of the portfolio according to agreed criteria in collaboration with the relevant stakeholders

- Through analyses, portfolio monitoring, stakeholder management and know-how transfer, the IT portfolio manager creates transparency and consistency as well as conformity between group strategies and the interests of the business units.

- Derivation of new projects and programs

Fig. 4.39 Portfolio manager

It can be assumed that only in large corporations will this number of over 30 roles for IT service management alone really be lived. In medium-sized companies, only a few roles are really necessary and make sense. These roles then take over parts of the other roles, since they do not have as much weight in the organization and therefore do not cost as much time.

The essential roles from the ITIL v4 context are the following (adapted from [6]):

Incident Manager

The incident manager is responsible for the effective execution of the incident management process and performs the appropriate reporting.

PMO (Project Management Office)

Job Objectives:

- Tracking of budget and time for all IT projects

- Contact person for all project stakeholders

Tasks

- Responsible for the creation, maintenance and training as well as for all questions regarding the IT project management procedure model.

- Maintenance and creation of all templates and documents for IT project management

- Tracking of project goals and project meetings / milestones

- Tracking of budget and time for all IT projects

- Sparring partner for IT project managers

- Set-up and maintenance as well as tracking of project portfolio management / information and provision of PPM to management

Fig. 4.40 PMO (project management office)

First Level Support
The first level support agent registers and classifies incoming fault messages and attempts to resolve them immediately in order to restore the defined operating status of a service as quickly as possible.

Second Level Support
The second level support agent takes over fault messages from first level support which the latter cannot solve independently. The aim is to restore the defined operating status of a service as quickly as possible.

Change Manager
The change manager authorizes and documents all changes to the IT infrastructure and its components (configuration items) in order to minimize disruptive effects on ongoing operations.

Release Manager
The release manager is responsible for planning and monitoring the transfer of releases to the test and live environments.

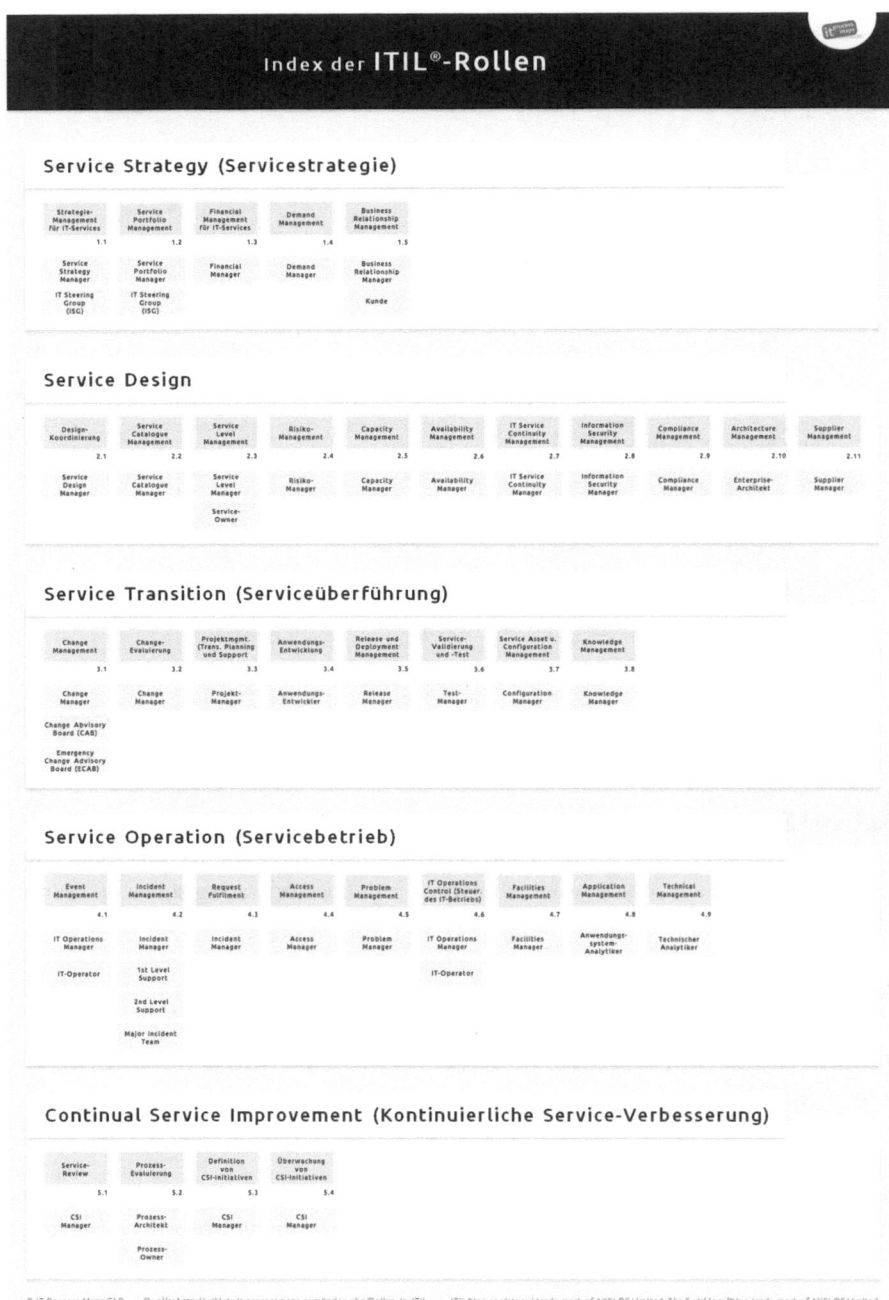

Fig. 4.41 Overview of all ITIL roles (ITIL v4)

4.4.8   IT Operations

The following roles are important in IT operations:

- Application administrator/manager.
- System administrator.
- Operator.
- Workstation technician.
- Employees service desk.
- IT service desk manager.
- IT quality manager.
- IT service manager.

A more detailed job description is not provided here, as these are presented very clearly in the ITIL role model mentioned above.

4.4.9   Interfaces and Decision Rights of the IT Roles

To make the interfaces and decision rights of the described roles clear, a so-called RACI matrix can be very helpful. RACI means:

- Responsible: You are responsible in the sense of being responsible for implementation, i.e., you then actively carry out this task.
- Accountable: You are accountable, i.e., responsible, for the costs or the entire topic.
- Consulted: These are the people who are then consulted on questions, on specific topics.
- Informed: These individuals or these roles are to be informed when this process step or activity occurs.

Structure of the RACI Matrix.

And you can imagine a RACI matrix as a classic table in which you first list the individual tasks on the left-hand side and then list all the roles on the horizontal at the top and then assign in this matrix, so to speak, which role has an R, an A, a C, or an I in which task.

In this way, you can actually visualize quite quickly how the responsibilities are divided. That means, with this RACI matrix, you have a tool, a mechanism, on how you can visualize quite quickly how the responsibilities should actually look like. And you can then leave them according to this matrix.

References

1. ISACA: "COBIT 5: Rahmenwerk für Governance und Management der Unternehmens-IT", abgerufen unter isaca.org durch Anmeldung als Member. Abgerufen am 15.01.2020.
2. Capgemini: "IT-Trends 2019", https://www.capgemini.com/de-de/wp-content/uploads/sites/5/2019/02/IT-Trends-Studie-2019.pdf, abgerufen am 28.12.2019.
3. AXELOS/TSO (The Stationery Office): "ITIL Foundation, ITIL v4", 1. Auflage, AXELOS/TSO 2019.
4. Gadatsch, A.: IT-Controlling, Praxiswissen für IT-Controller und Chief Information Officer, 1. Auflage, Springer Verlag, 2012.
5. Urbach, Ahlemann: (2017). Die IT-Organisation im Wandel: Implikationen der Digitalisierung für das IT-Management. HMD Praxis der Wirtschaftsinformatik. 54. 300–312.
6. Kempter, Andrea und Kempter, Stefan: "Rollen it ITIL | IT-Process-Map", https://wiki.de.it-processmaps.com/index.php/Rollen_in_ITIL, abgerufen am 29.12.2019.

Part III

The Role of IT and the CIO in the Company

The Role of IT in the Company

5

Abstract

IT is one of the key success factors for companies in the digital age. In this chapter, the drivers and influencing factors for an IT organization are presented, and the new role of IT in a digital world is also described in detail on the basis of an assessment of the current situation and the expectations of IT.

5.1 Drivers and Influencing Factors of the IT Organization

Before the role of IT in the company can be defined, it must be clear what the drivers and factors are that influence an IT organization in today's world. The IT organization faces a variety of challenges – both from the outside in the form of market pressure and from the inside through the business departments and the management. The following five challenges stand out in the 2020s:

- Digitalization and new digital business models.
- Agility, dynamism, and collaborative working.
- Consumerization of IT and IT security.
- Artificial intelligence, IoT, and cloud computing.
- Finding and retaining talent and experts.

In the following, these challenges are examined in more detail with regard to the potential for change for IT.

5.1.1   Digitization and New Digital Business Models

As shown in Fig. 5.1, digitization can be differentiated on three levels:

- Digital processes.
- Digital products.
- Digital business models.

In the lower field of the figure, the role of IT is shown in each case, and the goals and examples for these three levels of digitization are depicted. In this context, it is always important to ask "Who in the company has to deal with digitalization on which level and who has which role?" because, even though everyone is affected, responsibilities must be clear even in the digital age.

Digital processes have basically always existed – hence, the addition of 4.0, which was obviously preceded by 1.0 and 2.0. These are the reasons for the typical automation and process optimization topics. Basically, it has always been the task of IT to drive automation forward. This has been and continues to be done in close coordination with the process managers or department heads.

At the level of digital products, new technologies such as sensors have enabled extensive connectivity and new "smart" functions for some time. Products are networked, can communicate with each other, or become "smart" through sensor technology or electronics. This is the primary task of the product management or technical development or R&D department. IT is also important here because it provides the necessary apps and service portals for controlling and managing smart and networked products.

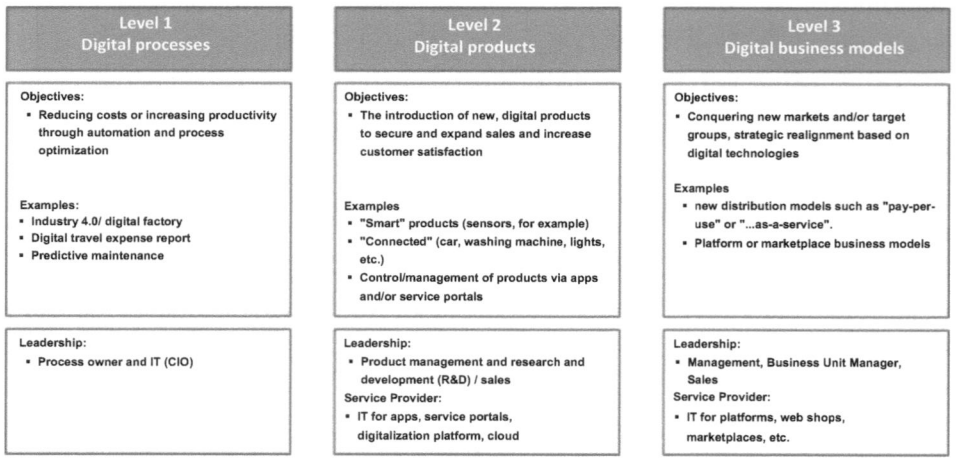

Fig. 5.1 The three levels of digitization

The topic of "digital business models" is indeed a "game changer," because, at this level, new business models and sales approaches are emerging through clever use of new technologies that can be truly revolutionary – see the platform examples Airbnb (largest landlord without owning hotels or houses) and Uber (largest mobility provider without owning cars, etc.). This is where the board and top management really need to understand the new opportunities that new technologies present. Platforms, marketplaces, but also distribution models like "pay-per-use" or "…as-a-service" can really take the existing business to a new level. Here, IT is in the role of the service provider for the development and operation of new platforms or the mapping of new sales models in existing systems.

It remains to be said that digital products and new digital business models alone place completely new demands on IT. And in addition to the apps, service portals, and platforms described above, which have to be planned, developed, and operated, IT plays a very important role on another level: It is not only the technical developer and operator of these systems but also a partner and advisor for the management and product management. Moreover, IT is increasingly becoming an integral part of the product. For example, the car connected to the Internet, the so-called connected car, is a good example of the fact that cars will be small, rolling data centers in the future. Technical development or product management still take on many of the actual IT tasks, but in the future, IT and its CIO will have to take on much more responsibility here. IT will move from being a service provider for the provision of ERP systems to becoming a real designer of the product and developer of new business models. A completely new role!

5.1.2 Agility, Dynamism, and Collaborative Working

Digitization and its technological leaps have also completely changed the way we work and collaborate (see Sect. 9.1.2 for a detailed description of the changes in the world of work in the context of leadership agility).

In the industrial age, Taylorism, using Ford as an example, was characterized by assembly line work and piecework wages. Relatively dull work had to be done, and the brain could be handed in at the factory gate. This is undergoing a radical change, because IT in particular is primarily about ever new knowledge services. IT employees are knowledge workers and no longer want to be trapped in rigid time and wage constructs from the industrial past. However, many manufacturing companies still find this very difficult today. The world is also changing radically at the level of leadership: from the command and control of the industrial era to management by objectives (MbO) and mentoring in the knowledge age. Many IT managers still have a hard time with this, because they "learned" it differently in the 1990s and 2000s.

Radical changes are also taking place at the level of process models. One example is the waterfall model that many people are still familiar with, with its eternally long requirements and functional specifications. This is no longer imaginable today. A requirements specification with more than 200 or 300 pages probably needs a year to be finally approved by umpteen instances. The content would already be outdated in this day and age. This is why SCRUM and other agile methods have taken hold (see Sect. 5.4 for details).

For IT and those responsible for it, this change means rethinking at almost all levels, from management to process models, and the world is just changing from the somewhat unwieldy industrial way of working to a knowledge economy with completely different laws.

5.1.3   Consumerization of IT and IT Security

IT is now commonplace in the private lives of all users. Every employee has at least one smartphone and a PC or notebook as well as a tablet. They know the latest apps and are aware of innovations in the IT industry. In the 1990s, this was the job of IT, but today, many IT departments struggle to keep up with users. Of course, the IT employee cannot know every app, but the overall requirements have grown enormously.

In addition, employees and users at work want to be able to use their company mobile phones and PCs just as freely as they do in their private lives. Security concerns are often diametrically opposed to free use. How should IT react to this? What may be allowed, what must be blocked, and why?

IT and cybersecurity are very serious topics, as they can cause companies in today's world to disappear from the market overnight due to problems in this area. In the past, the company had to be physically broken into; today, the next hacker attack can threaten from anywhere in the world, stealing company secrets or crippling the entire company. Here, too, IT must find responsible, accountable solutions and fulfill its role as a modern shaper and guardian of data worth protecting.

5.1.4   Artificial Intelligence, IoT, and Cloud Computing

New technologies such as artificial intelligence or IoT are very valuable tools at application level in existing or new IT systems. Examples include predictive maintenance or machine-to-machine communication. These are beneficial additions for companies.

On another level, these new technologies mean that IT no longer takes place in the IT department at all, but in the specialist department itself. Cloud computing, such as Salesforce, means that the sales department no longer needs IT. The program no longer has to run on a server in the company's own data center after it has been installed there by IT; instead, the sales employee buys the license on the Internet and can get started immediately. This presents IT with completely different challenges. Because at the latest when such cloud applications grow, customizing becomes necessary and especially when interfaces to existing IT systems become necessary, IT has to help again. This also means a new role for IT: It is no longer needed as a service provider but must still ensure that the system landscape remains manageable. Making everyone aware of this role is often difficult enough.

5.1.5 Finding and Retaining Talent and Experts

In order to meet the extensive new challenges, good personnel in IT is indispensable. Unfortunately, there is still a shortage here in Germany. Many young people still shy away from studying IT, and those who do have the knowledge do not want to work in rigid structures from the old industrial age. Not only IT but also HR must find new solutions here. HR marketing is one of the big and important fields, and social media should definitely be used as an important channel to potential IT experts. Also internal bonuses for advertising an acquaintance or relative can be very helpful in the recruitment phase. In any case, finding as well as keeping IT experts decides to a large extent on the success of your IT and thus of the entire company.

5.2 Positioning: Where Does IT Stand Today?

In order to determine the current role of IT in the company, it helps to look at how IT is seen in the company, what role it plays, and why, in the form of a reflection.

Figure 5.2 shows the typical five development stages of IT – from the so-called technology professional to a possible role of "IT as a business model." It is not to be judged as good or bad on which level one's own IT is located, but it depends on the company's purpose and envisaged goals on which level the IT should be located.

The following questions for reflection help to clearly identify your own starting situation and your own role as IT and CIO:

IT Organisational form	Recognizable by.
Stage I: IT as technology professionals	▸ IT as technology gurus/nerds who are in love with themselves (preferably no customer contact) ▸ Often classic IT organization (two teams: application development and IT infrastructure)
Stage II: IT as a service provider	▸ Developing DL mentality without own strategy and not at eye level with business ▸ Often Plan-Build-Run
Stage III: IT as a business partner	▸ Strong DL mentality with strategy and for the first time at eye level with business ▸ Distinct plan with possibly demand function
Stage IV: IT as a business innovator	▸ Strong IT. that drives the business at eye level with the business ▸ Demand/Supply with strong Biz integration
Stage V: IT as a business(model)	▸ IT is part of the business model ▸ IT is divided into "internal/Corp IT" and "IT R&D" as product/service developer

Fig. 5.2 The five stages of IT from technology professional to IT as a business model

- What level am I currently at?
- What does this mean for me and IT?
- Can steps be skipped or must they be climbed one step at a time?
- At what level does management want to see IT?
- Do you see it the same way, and how much effort will it take to get from where we are today to where we want to be?

The answer to this question is immensely important for the classification of the initial situation. This in turn is an important foundation and starting point for achieving the IT vision that is subsequently developed.

5.3   Clarify Expectations of the IT Organization

In addition to determining where your IT stands, it is very important to identify what is expected of IT. The following questions can be helpful in determining expectations:

- Who in management is particularly IT or digital savvy and wants to have a say?
- What are the topics that are currently burning under the nails of the management or the board of directors?
- Which are the biggest "requirements departments," i.e., where do most of the requirements for IT come from and why?
- What is the reputation of IT in the company and with which stakeholders is it best and with whom is it worst and why?
- How great is the appreciation and recognition of IT and its achievements?
- What does the owner, the shareholder, or the financial investor think about IT, and how important are IT issues to them for the future?

The IT organization is subject to manifold challenges – both from the outside in the form of market pressure and from the inside by the business departments and the management. Possible ideas and typical answers to the question of what is expected of IT can be the following:

- *Improved cost efficiency*: Due to the continuing high speed of innovation in the IT industry, there is a constant need for capital in the IT organization; in addition, know-how must be continuously renewed or purchased.
- *Customer orientation*: The integration of IT into the corporate hierarchy is becoming increasingly difficult (the role of IT in the company is sometimes unclear, and the responsibility for IT at the top of the company is often perceived by the CFO or commercial manager with a pure focus on finance/costs).
- *What is the value contribution to the company's success?*

- *Time to market*: Why is the flexibility and agility in IT not so high that requirements can finally be implemented faster?
- *Service quality and availability*: Why is it not possible in times of "IT as a commodity" – similar to electricity from the socket – that IT performances and services are available around the clock in a stable and reliable manner?

It has already been mentioned in the questions, and it makes sense to take a closer look at the stakeholders. A simple stakeholder analysis can serve this purpose.

Step 1: Identification of all Relevant Stakeholders
The first step is to develop a list of all stakeholders relevant to IT. The overview of possible stakeholders for IT shown in Fig. 5.3 can provide an initial overview.

This is a large group of people who have expectations of IT and its leader or CIO. It is important to distinguish between the expectations of the function or role and the expectations of the person who takes on that role or function. This is because the expectations of the function/role can be entirely different than the expectations of the individual. Nevertheless, managers in the company are bound by the expectations placed on them through their role.

So how do you go about analyzing expectations?

A stakeholder analysis is not a task that is completed within an hour, but one that is continually filled in. In the first days and weeks, the pieces of the mosaic come together to form an increasingly clear picture.

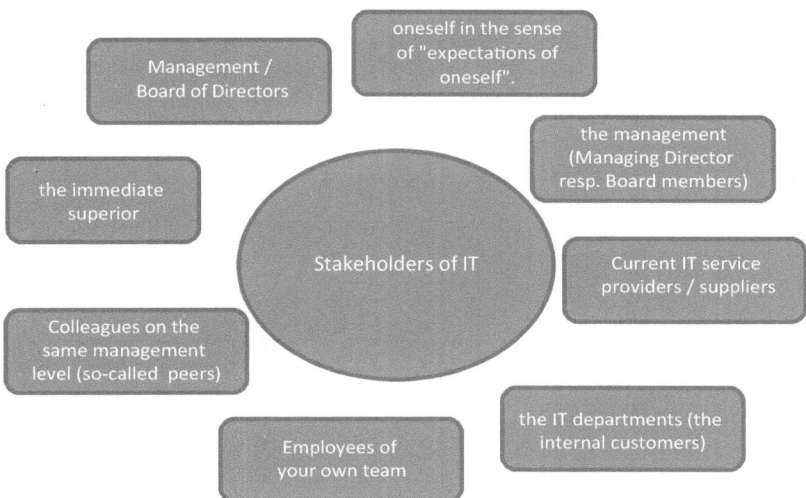

Fig. 5.3 Possible group of relevant stakeholders for IT

Based on the nine stakeholder groups shown in the diagram, the individual stakeholders must now be identified. In order to capture all stakeholders, it helps in this first phase to ask yourself questions such as:

- Who needs IT solutions?
- Who benefits greatly from good IT services?
- Who is afraid of possible IT projects or their effects?
- Is there anyone who is constantly upset about IT?
- Who is responsible for the IT budget?
- Who can hope to win management or shareholder laurels on the basis of IT?
- Which suppliers or service providers are necessary or involved and what is their intention?

Each stakeholder is entered into an Excel spreadsheet.

Step 2: Write Down the Expectations and Make an Assessment
Now the evaluation of each person is done according to the following three criteria:

- Stakeholder influence (from 1 = very high to 5 = very low).
- Stakeholder expectations (1 = very high to 5 = very low).
- Interest in the success of IT (1 = very high to 5 = very low).

This evaluation is entered into the Excel list and looks exemplary as in Fig. 5.4.

Step 3: Make Decisions About Managing Expectations
After the assessments are made, there is an evaluation of the expectation and how to deal with it. The following steps are helpful for this:

No.	Name	Function / Role	Influence of the Stakeholders	Expectations of the Stakeholders	Interest in the IT success	Specific expectations	Possible measures
			1 = very low 2 = low 3 = medium 4 = large 5 = very large	1 = very low 2 = low 3 = medium 4 = large 5 = very large	1 = very low 2 = low 3 = neutral 4 = high 5 = very high		
1	Max Mustermann	chief financial officer	5	3	4	Finally reports with all Key financial figures for all locations	Expectation cannot be fulfilled immediately; coordination and explanation necessary
2	Maxi sample woman	IT Service Manager	2	4	4	Recognition for the work of the IT infrastructure; more budget for servers	Promote recognition through IT Ops meeting; arguments for more budget are not clear; vote needed.
3							
4							
5							

Fig. 5.4 Note the expectations of the stakeholders

- Marking expectations that can be met well (strengths) and those that are difficult (weaknesses).
- Consider expectations that are difficult to fulfill and think about possible solutions. Here it makes sense to limit oneself to three expectations at first.
- Now it is necessary to check which can and should expectations contradict one's own values and goals.
- What are the consequences of not meeting these expectations? It is important to look for solutions and to reconcile one's own expectations with those of others or at least to mitigate unpleasant consequences.
- Own solution approaches: Three expectations that are difficult to meet, especially with must and should expectations.
- What do you not want to fulfill yourself? – Can and should expectations that contradict one's own values and goals and possible solutions to avoid conflicts.

The overall evaluation is automatically generated from the Excel file based on the evaluation and is exemplified in Fig. 5.5.

Here, the circumference or volume of the circle corresponds to the interest in the success of IT. The other two evaluation criteria are shown as x- and y-axis (x = influence and y = expectation).

Reflection Questions on the Largest Stakeholder Groups in the Overview
Reflection questions for management:

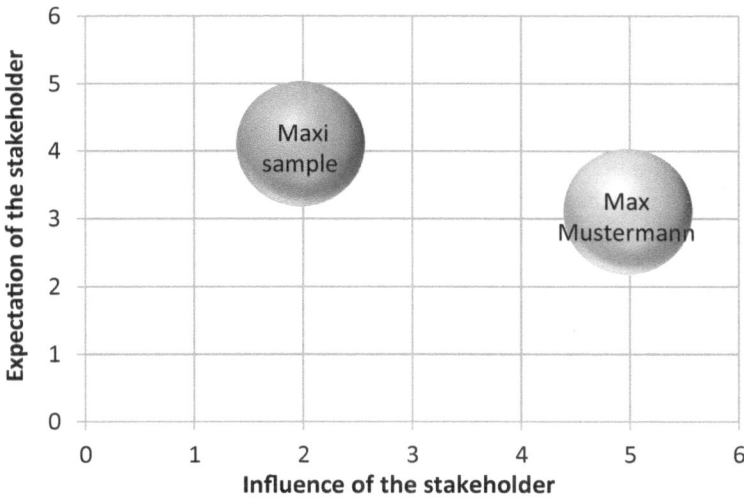

Fig. 5.5 Overview of the results of the stakeholder analysis

- What is really important to management in terms of IT?
- What role should IT play from the management's point of view?
- What have been the "pain points" so far in terms of IT and how can we do better?

Questions about the direct supervisor:

- What values – apart from loyalty – are particularly important to one's own superior when it comes to working together?
- To what extent does the superior want to have a say in the strategy and management of IT and how much freedom do you have yourself?
- Who represents IT and its concerns in the management? You as CIO or your supervisor?
- Are there unspoken expectations?

Questions to colleagues at the same management level (peers):

- Who is the "secret" leader at the peer level?
- Which of the peers is "good" with IT and which is more "bad" and why is that?
- Listening carefully and having one-on-one conversations helps to understand the power structure and "who with whom?"
- Where is there or can there be a tussle of competencies (CIO versus CDO or CMO)?

In this way, IT can become a connecting element between the corporate strategy, the specialist departments, and the customers and thus contribute to the development of the networked unit or shape it significantly. This interaction between business and IT takes IT out of the role of the driven and helps companies as a whole to survive successfully in the market.

5.4   The New Role of IT: Old Ways of Thinking Must Be Overcome

IT in companies has been subject to a great deal of constant change in recent years due to the advancing "mechanization" of business models. No other organizational unit has changed so much in recent years due to the ever-faster technology life cycle. Ever new technology hype ensures that companies can work even more efficiently, that processes can be automated even more, and that information can be evaluated even better.

Figure 5.6 shows how IT can assert itself in this strong change through technology and what role IT can and should take in this context. Depicted on two levels or axes, IT can take on the following roles:

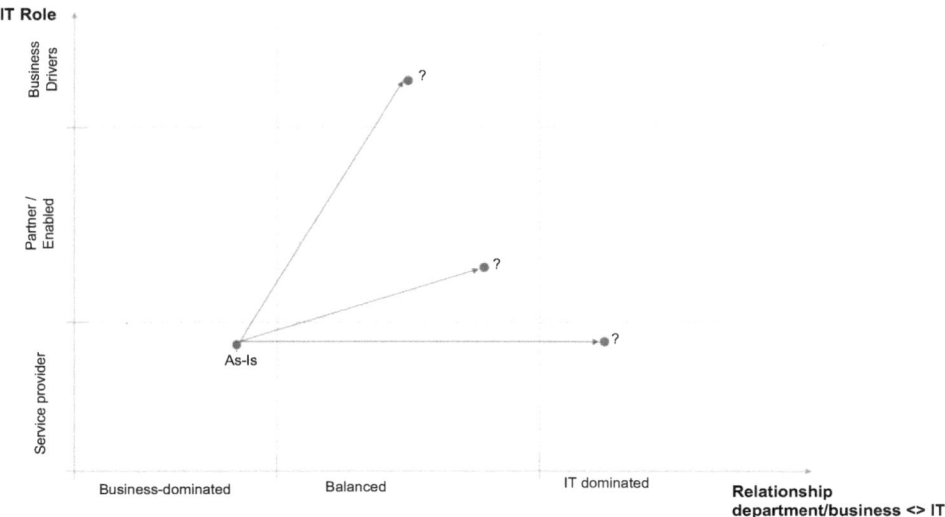

Fig. 5.6 Overview of the role of IT

- The role of IT either as:
  - Service provider.
  - Partner/enabler.
  - Business drivers.
- The relationship between business and IT:
  - Business-dominated.
  - Balanced.
  - IT dominated.

As an example, Fig. 5.6 shows that IT currently finds itself in the role of service provider and is rather business-dominated. The question now arises as to how such IT can develop further and what could possibly be a more suitable role for the company? Three scenarios are shown in the figure as examples.

Scenario 1: IT Becomes the Business Driver and the Relationship Between Business and IT Is Balanced
In this example, IT changes its role relatively radically and even skips a phase, namely, that of partner or enabler. What does the role of IT as a business driver mean? As a service provider, IT is heavily dependent on business units, their requirements, and wishes. The result of this is usually highly customized IT systems that have been adapted to the individual wishes of the business departments. This leads to expensive maintenance and update efforts. IT becomes slow, and the business departments are increasingly annoyed by the slow and expensive IT, even though it was their wishes outside the standard that led

to this. In contrast, in the role of business driver, IT itself takes ownership and ensures that projects and initiatives are launched that add value closely aligned to business goals and create real value for the business. When setting up and introducing new IT systems, IT takes the reins, leads change processes, and thus drives the business in the right direction for the company. In addition, IT and its management team are closely involved in the formulation of new corporate strategies and develop approaches for additive business models based on new technologies. IT thus assumes real responsibility for the positive development of the business and thus of the company.

Scenario 2: IT Becomes a Partner with an Equally Balanced Relationship Between Business and IT
In the second example, IT becomes a partner with a balanced relationship between business and IT. This partner role is also referred to as an enabler. This means that IT empowers the company and the business units to identify and see new business models and opportunities that further increase the company's value. IT takes on a kind of consulting role, no longer just providing services, but looking for possible solutions at eye level with the business units and actively coming up with suggestions and ideas from IT. In this sense, IT can also become a true partner for many initiatives and projects in the area of digital transformation.

Scenario 3: IT Remains Service Provider, But the Relationship Between Business and IT Is Dominated by IT
In this scenario, IT remains true to its role as a service provider, but the decisions about the implementation and feasibility of IT projects are now the responsibility of IT and no longer of the business departments. IT increasingly assumes a role that does not interfere with the business but instead sets much stronger priorities and takes on leadership at the level of requirements and projects. It remains true to itself as a service provider but is growing into a role that sets clear guidelines, for example, on the development plan and on the approach and methodology for projects. It also sets clear guidelines on IT security and cloud strategies that are not questioned by the business departments. You grow within your service provider role and can consciously act more strongly there instead of always just reacting to the requirements of the departments.

5.4.1   From Administrator of Technology to Designer of Digital Change

As already roughly illustrated in scenario 1, in many companies, IT is changing its role from a service provider with rather technical roots to a business driver and shaper of the digital transformation. In order to be able to assume this new position in the company and to successfully navigate the path to this position, one thing is particularly important: Old thought patterns must be overcome.

What does that mean?

As already outlined in Sect. 5.1, the major drivers and influencing factors for companies and IT today are digitalization, new technologies such as AI, and the associated new requirements from customers, suppliers, and also employees (see new work, digital workplace, etc.).

What all these things have in common is that answers to questions about new sales channels, customer wishes, or the wishes of shareholders have to be met more quickly than before.

This has a huge impact on IT. Because of relatively rigid legacy systems, requirements and new functionalities are often difficult and time-consuming to implement. IT groans due to permanent overload, the departments or customers are frustrated by the lengthy implementation of requirements, and the management fears losing touch with the market and competitors.

The previous way of thinking about IT as a technology professional and pure service provider is no longer conceivable in this context, as this would have a massive impact on the success of the company.

The big question is therefore: How can IT become the shaper of change?

In fact, the most important means to do this is to change the mindset – the mindset of new organizations and responsibilities. It is so ingrained in the minds of employees and managers and thus in the DNA of a company that IT, with its technology professionals, provides services and operates them securely.

And IT itself has also internalized this pattern to such an extent that even IT employees think about themselves in this way. How can this thinking be dissolved and replaced by a new self-image?

A lot of communication and answering the "why" is needed here! Why should IT change at all? What is the benefit for the company and IT? These questions need to be discussed in the leadership circle and the management. And then, ideally, a story needs to be developed that is conveyed over and over again and that becomes so deeply ingrained in the minds of everyone involved that, after a while, no one asks why IT should care about change issues, business alignment, and strategic things in the meantime. It is just the way it is and it makes sense.

5.4.2   The Four Stages of IT Becoming an Innovation Driver

In the context of shaping change, the topic of innovation is at the top of the list. How can IT set the tone here and drive real innovation in the company?

An example can be given by the so-called IT Strategy 2.0 of BMW AG. It is based on four pillars [1]:

- Tech-driven products, processes, and services.
- Data- and technology-based business innovation.

- Stable and performant platforms and IT products.
- Empowered people and agile platforms.

To this end, BMW strategists have identified five game changers on which IT should focus in the coming years:

1. Data-driven company.
2. BizDevOps structures.
3. Cloud-based platforms.
4. IT security.
5. Internal software skills.

The latter are particularly important to the IT bosses. BMW wants to use this to strengthen the "core performance" of IT, i.e., above all to build up more know-how again in terms of software development within the group. To this end, former BMW CIO Klaus Straub had launched the Back2Code initiative and thus made a roll backward, which has been extraordinarily successful because finally everyone is talking to each other again on an equal technical footing.

5.4.3   Conflict Potential 1: "Sovereign Tasks" Versus Service Tasks

The company's system landscape and IT architecture can and must only be specified by IT. The same applies to IT security standards, because only the CIO and his team have the competence in the company to assess this conclusively and it is their very own job to ensure a functioning, scalable IT architecture and a high level of IT security.

The balance between the requirements of the employees and the resulting costs on the one hand and the security and scalability on the other hand must always be taken into account.

If IT assumes the role of a service provider that allows everything that employees or departments want, then the aforementioned sovereign tasks can no longer be performed. Therefore, the service provider role must always be subject to the restriction that services that are needed in the company are provided quickly, scalably, and as cost-effectively as possible. The issue of standards versus customizing often plays a role here. Many departments want their own solution, which then has to be developed individually at high cost. This desire is often opposed by the issue of costs, especially in the sense of subsequent costs such as maintenance and care, because, in the worst case, the individual development means that updates and release cycles are no longer possible to ensure that the software remains up to date.

Therefore, it is important for the management to recognize that IT and its CIO are service providers in the sense of a scalable and agile IT architecture and a secure system landscape for the company but logically cannot fulfill every wish 1:1. It is usually sufficient if this conflict potential is explained and recognized. Then the conflict is usually already resolved, because for most requesters, this sovereign task is comprehensible after explanation and therefore acceptable.

5.4.4   Conflict Potential 2: Self-Image Versus External Image

In addition, there are always different perspectives on the role. For example, the company management sees the role of IT as a service provider, but the CIO sees himself as a business innovator. Then the difference in the understanding of the role is great, and differences are inevitable. Therefore, aligning perspectives and discussing the right positioning of IT with management is very important for success – not only for the CIO but for the entire IT organization. Developing an IT strategy or IT roadmap can be an ideal approach to discuss IT's role in detail and define a common path to defining it in 3–5 years.

5.5   The New Role of IT Drives the Business: How IT Can Create Real Business Value

Based on the model of the development of IT in five stages (see Fig. 5.2), the implications of the changed role of IT for the company can be derived.

Figure 5.7 clearly shows how the change in the role of IT also transforms the company. This is of great interest and value not only for the CIO but also for the entire management.

Because, from the historically known stage I of "IT as technology professionals," little to no impetus came from IT into the company. In this phase, IT was usually ridiculed, and the IT colleagues were often dismissed as "nerds" with whom efficient business communication was not possible. At the business level, such companies often have a strongly

Fig. 5.7 How IT drives the business forward

hierarchical structure with a command and order management style or a "chaos structure" in which no one knows exactly what to do, because the lack of structures at the management level means that excessive demands are the order of the day. In stage II, in which IT functions as a service provider, IT takes on a stronger customer orientation for the first time, but is still not on an equal footing with the business departments and is still perceived by them as a support function. For the business, this step to level II means that project management and management based on objectives (management by objectives – MbO) are often more pronounced. Processes are also standardized for the first time.

Stage III is a big leap for IT onto the tableau of true eye level with the business units. IT is taken "seriously" and considered important, as it becomes clear for the first time that IT is very important for increasing efficiency and reducing costs in the company. At the business level, this becomes clear through a strong process competence in the form of process optimizations and re-engineering in order to implement the goals of increasing efficiency and reducing costs. Through large transformation projects, which are no longer understood as IT projects only, the readiness and reflection for changes and change management in the company through IT grow. At level IV, the strategic importance is also recognized in addition to the increase in efficiency. In this framework, IT grows even closer with the business units and has distinctive and very professional processes for implementing major transformations. At the business level, this new understanding of IT's role is reflected by a more pronounced awareness of innovation, a lot of collaboration, and agility. As a result, large transformations can be implemented much faster and more efficiently, and the customer focus becomes even more central. The final stage V of IT means a radical transformation of the company into a tech company. From a more process-driven way of doing business, the company is transforming into an IT-driven business model. Often this is combined with a very data-driven organization (data-driven company). Characteristics of such an organization are independence, constant innovation, entrepreneurial thinking, and agility.

Reference

1. *Herrmann, Wolfgang (Computerwoche)*: "BMW IT Strategie 2.0", https://www.cio.de/a/bmw-it-setzt-auf-mehr-eigenleistung,3625034, abgerufen am 15.01.2020.

Quo Vadis CIO? – The Role of the CIO in Times of Digital Transformation

6

Abstract

When IT takes on a new and increasingly important role in the company, this naturally has an impact on the role of the CIO! In addition to the description and definition of CIO role models, this chapter is primarily concerned with the new tasks of the CIO and the presentation of which skills and competencies a CIO must have in a modern company.

The role of the CIO is changing rapidly with the new purpose of IT: from the former cost center manager to a digital strategist with the task of driving innovation within the company.

The aforementioned transformation of the IT organization in the direction of the business is also changing the role of the CIO. Previously mostly technically oriented, managers are now in demand who understand the business precisely and are able to assess exactly where the added value lever for IT in the company should be applied.

It is clear that the challenges facing the CIO and his or her organization will continue to evolve at the same pace as new technologies create new opportunities for business innovation.

The further development and thus competitiveness of the company are therefore just as much his responsibility as that of his colleagues on the business side. He is challenged not only as an expert for new technologies but also as a leader who moves the company forward.

On this basis, a closer look will be taken at which CIO role models exist, what the tasks of the CIO are, and how these have changed. This also includes taking a closer look at the skills and competencies required today. Finally, a comparison between CDO and CIO will follow in order to delineate who is actually responsible for the digital transformation now.

© The Author(s), under exclusive license to Springer Fachmedien Wiesbaden GmbH, part of Springer Nature 2024
V. Johanning, *Organization and Management of IT*,
https://doi.org/10.1007/978-3-658-39572-8_6

6.1   CIO Role Models

The role of the CIO, however, continues to change: There are signs of a shift from "technical implementer" to "shaper of digital change," who is seen as a partner and enabler of the business at eye level. This also changes the role of the CIO in the overall context of the company. Table 6.1, based on Brenner [1], shows this change in the role of the CIO.

First of all, it should be noted that, in the following, the role of the CIO is used synonymously with the terms IT manager, CTO (chief technology officer), or EDP manager, which are also commonly used in the market. As we have seen in the context of developing demand/supply structures, there is a difference between the CIO and CTO in that the CIO leads the demand arm and the CTO leads the supply arm as the "IT factory." This differentiation is important for the Demand/Supply structure, but here we are talking about the person who reports directly to senior management, and that is usually the CIO or the IT director. It should also be mentioned that in the demand/supply structure, the CTO reports to the CIO and the CIO reports to the management.

What are the main tasks of a CIO? Analogous to the cross-sectional functions as described in the Demand/Supply construct, these are primarily the following areas:

* IT strategy (alignment of corporate and IT strategy, strategic orientation of IT).
* IT architecture (creating standards and economies of scale in the context of development plans).
* Leading the IT organization (IT leadership and governance).
* Management of external suppliers (provider management).
* Portfolio planning and prioritization.
* Risk management and IT security.

In addition to this list of main tasks of a CIO, three roles can be distinguished, which are aptly depicted on Wikipedia and are presented in Table 6.2.

Table 6.1 Change in the role of the CIO

Old role	New role
Technology-oriented	Business model and process oriented
IT as content	IT as a means to an end
Technically qualified	Leadership qualified
Specialist	Generalist
Think in terms of cost	Think in terms of results
Internally oriented	Externally oriented
Knows technology	Knows technology and business

Source: Brenner et al. [1]

Table 6.2 Three possible roles of a CIO

Role	Description of the role
"Run the business" (operational functions)	The basic tasks of an IT manager: Ensuring the smooth operation of the IT system and supporting the IT infrastructure. Due to the high level of dependency and the influence of IT on all other areas of the company, ensuring the functionality of the IT system in the company is considered a fundamental task. This also includes ensuring that the IT system meets the requirements of the users in terms of quality, service, and availability. The CIO must coordinate and manage the use of technology capabilities to improve operational and service processes. He or she is also responsible for promoting the flow of information across the company as well as interconnectedness and data sharing within the company. At the same time, it is also important to ensure that everyone's data is protected. In general, the security of the entire IT system must be guaranteed at a high level. It is thus responsible for providing a reliable and secure information technology system to enable efficient operation of the business. This is especially important to build trust in IT and provide transparency. All of this must be provided at a reasonable cost by the IT department
"Change the business" (innovation management)	The CIO must demonstrate the possibilities of modern ICT for the company and constantly drive innovations so that the existing potential for improvement can be exploited. To do this, he must monitor the current developments of potentially relevant technical innovations and then assess their significance for the company. He must then provide the impetus for new technology projects. It is also the IT manager's job to find the right timing for the introduction of technical innovations. All of this must be specifically adapted to one's own company so that technical innovations can actually be used in a way that adds value. Then, the right use of new technologies must be supported and monitored. It must consistently integrate new technologies that create value for the company into the existing company portfolio
"Engineer the business" (business efficiency and strategic consulting)	The IT manager is jointly responsible for the efficient design of the company. For this, he analyzes various possibilities on the basis of IT. For example, the value of individual areas or processes in the company can be determined or the potential increase in value through new opportunities. This can contribute to "make-or-buy" questions. To do this, a CIO must have a good understanding of the structures and interrelationships within the company. He thus has an advisory function for the management. To do this, he needs a comprehensive understanding of current market trends. He identifies opportunities for competitive differentiation. In this way, future business areas can be identified for the company. The existing sales and distribution channels can be revamped or new ones developed if necessary. This allows him to identify future technology directions and priorities that are important for increasing the value of the company. The development and adaptation of IT strategies must in each case be carried out in accordance with the business strategy, although it is equally possible that business strategies can only be developed or refined on the basis of new ICT potential. The necessary strategies, information, experience, methods, and IT support must be made available for implementation in the respective areas

Source: Taken from Wikipedia [2]

The approach outlined in Wikipedia very clearly shows the transformation of the CIO's role from technician ("Run the Business") to IT manager at eye level with the company management. He not only masters the technology but also knows the business and can thus use IT even more efficiently as an innovation driver ("Change the Business") or even for the purpose of actual value enhancement as a strategic consultant ("Engineer the Business").

6.2   Tasks of a CIO: Working *on* IT and Not *in* IT

When looking at the tasks of a CIO, it is helpful to take a brief look at the last two decades. That is because CIOs still often focus on technology. Until now, his essential task has been to provide IT and keep it running so that the actual value-creating processes in the company are optimally supported.

When it comes to the duties of the CIO, a quick look back to the 2000s is very helpful. The tasks in the 2000s can be summarized like this:

- CIOs are responsible for reactive demand management. They take requirements from the business units, channel them, and harmonize them.
- CIOs are responsible for the entire IT infrastructure: from the servers in the data center and the networks to the databases and the individual applications. This also includes IT security and IT support.
- CIOs develop the IT infrastructure with the aim of ensuring business continuity – for example, new releases of existing solutions.
- CIOs are partly responsible for the analysis and design of business processes in order to be able to map them on the IT side.
- CIOs continue to develop the IT infrastructure in order to continuously optimize and automate all business processes and to meet business requirements. This also involves best-of-breed solutions that address very specific requirements.
- CIOs lead team leaders from IT development, technical administration, and technical support.
- CIOs are responsible for quality assurance and project management.
- CIOs are responsible for defining and implementing IT investments, including IT support for internal users.

These specific requirements have resulted in a typical profile that CIOs have had to meet in the past (again, looking back to the 2000s):

- CIOs have successfully completed a degree in computer science or business informatics.
- CIOs draw on several years of professional experience in IT development or IT governance – including leadership experience.
- CIOs have deep IT expertise and hands-on experience in networking.

- CIOs have extensive programming experience.
- CIOs have very good analytical and communication skills, implementation strength, and initiative.
- CIOs have very good project management skills and experience in large IT projects.

If we look at the present in the early 2020s, then this task and requirement profile of the CIO has changed very significantly. Digitization with its game changers artificial intelligence, IoT, its dynamics, and agile way of working requires a new range of tasks and, above all, places different demands on the CIO than before.

You can sum it up with the following sentence:

Today's CIO No Longer Has to Work in IT, But *on* IT!
An article from the magazine *Computerwoche* puts it in a nutshell [3].

So instead of managing everything to do with IT, the CIO today must:

- Anticipate the added value and importance of new technologies for the company as a whole.
- Agree standards and structures for data integration with business units so that different technologies can communicate and access data together.
- Define and implement standards for data security.
- Provide end-to-end service levels.

It is clear that the challenges facing the CIO and his or her organization will continue to evolve at the same pace as new technologies create new opportunities for business innovation.

The further development and thus competitiveness of the company are therefore just as much his responsibility as that of his colleagues on the business side. He is challenged not only as an expert for new technologies but also as a leader who moves the company forward.

Figure 6.1 shows the change in the CIO role on the basis of his tasks, which were previously always strongly characterized by reacting and are now merging into an acting role.

6.3   Necessary Skills and Competencies of the CIO

The new role of the CIO requires new skills.

In addition to the topic of "new leadership," another four topics rank high on the agenda of the skills needed by a future-ready CIO:

1. Agile leadership: modern leadership instead of command and control.
2. Managing and leading change: not just making the technology work, but the people and the processes.

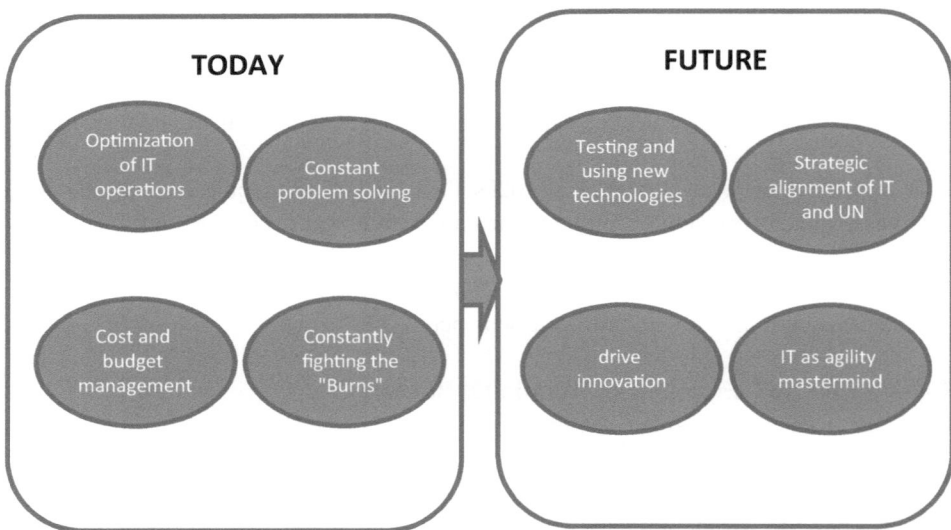

Fig. 6.1 Acting instead of reacting

3. Entrepreneurial thinking: making clear the business impact and benefits of IT.
4. Communication and marketing: making IT understandable.
5. Simplify complexity: understand technologies and use them correctly for the company.

6.3.1   Agile Leadership: Modern Leadership Instead of Command and Control

Leadership is becoming a more important topic, not only because command and order and pure management by objectives (MbO) have already exceeded their limits but also because the new generation of IT experts can choose where and how they want to work. It is not possible to recruit the next generation of IT experts without them, which is why agile leadership is so important. This also includes the form of mentoring and coaching of IT employees in the sense of "challenge and encourage."

6.3.2   The CIO as a Change Leader: Not Just Making the Technology Work, But the People and the Processes

CIOs need a good level of knowledge in the areas of change management, dealing with conflicts and resistance, as well as a well-functioning self-reflection.

Why is this so important today? The introduction of IT systems is primarily about managing change processes. You can quickly get to grips with the technology behind it, but all the "trappings" of rolling planning, agile methodologies, changes to the workflows of employees and users, and the associated adjustments to role descriptions or jobs that are eliminated through automation present the CIO with completely different tasks than managing the technology. The inherent complexity of such projects and the potential for conflict are also very high and represent an unusual hurdle for any CIO. However, good CIOs have to overcome these hurdles, which is why change management skills have become so immensely important.

6.3.3   Entrepreneurial Thinking: Demonstrating the Business Impact and Benefits of IT

It is nice when the new IT system and the IT as such function well in the sense of being stable and cost-effective and possibly even scalable. In the past, that was what CIOs were expected to do. Today, the focus is on the benefits and added value of IT and its systems. Only that which offers the company a real market advantage will win in the future. This presents the CIO with new challenges: He has to deal more with business cases, has to make the added value transparent to the management and defend it, and also has the task of identifying new business potential through new technologies and introducing them for the company.

6.3.4   Communication and Marketing: Making IT Understandable

Even if the added value has been understood and the technology and operations are running smoothly and are scalable so that everything is possible for the future, it is not yet said that IT and the CIO have done their job completely and to everyone's satisfaction. The point is that the CIO needs to be transparent about the new technologies, digitization, and both benefits to the business – transparent in the sense that the management, but also the business departments, understands how these things can be used, which advantages and disadvantages have to be considered, and what this means for their business. That is the role of the enabler. This is also helped by a fair amount of marketing understanding to use in their own interest. Roadshows, newsletters, communication events, and other marketing activities can help the CIO and IT be seen in a new light. This is imperative in order to be heard as an enabler.

6.3.5   Simplify Complexity: Understanding Technologies and Using Them Correctly for the Company

In the context of the CIO as enabler, this last point plays an important role: The CIO must simplify complexity. The world seems to have become more complex, more opaque. New technologies reach application maturity but often pose more questions than they provide answers. This is where the CIO comes in. It is his task to provide answers and to explain new technologies but also new business models that arise from them. The CIO must be able to show how it works and what added value it brings to the company. It is also his job to show what is possible and what is not. It is also up to him to illustrate what really makes sense and benefits the company and what perhaps should not be used, even though it is currently hype and many others are using it. Here, the CIO must actively become an enabler who understands things himself and can then teach them to others. In addition, he must be able to provide an explanation as to why something makes sense or not.

6.3.6   The Seven-Point Plan for Success as a CIO

Based on the EKS (bottleneck-focused strategy according to Prof. Mewes), the following seven steps are crucial for the CIO's success:

1. Finding your own bottlenecks.
2. Finding out the most burning problem of the departments and the company.
3. Aligning the benefits of IT with the burning problem.
4. Working out the strategy and vision of IT with management.
5. Living and developing the new role.
6. Seeking and retaining allies.
7. Developing an innovation strategy.

6.4   CIO Versus CDO: The CIO in the Digital Age

Unlike the CIO, the CDO is much more actively involved in the development of the company. He or she is expected to play a key role in shaping the digital transformation at the level of the organization, the processes, and the technology. To do this, he or she must keep an eye on market developments and customer wishes and understand them in order to draw the right conclusions for the company's products and services. At the same time, he must consider the consequences that result for the company and the IT infrastructure.

Figure 6.2 shows the differences and similarities in the tasks and requirements of the CDO versus the CIO.

Similar to the CIO in the previous chapter, the tasks of the CDO will be presented here in an overview:

• CDOs constantly analyze all time-relevant aspects, and they keep an eye on the dynamics and constancy of trends and changes in the corporate environment.
• CDOs critically evaluate and prioritize market requirements.

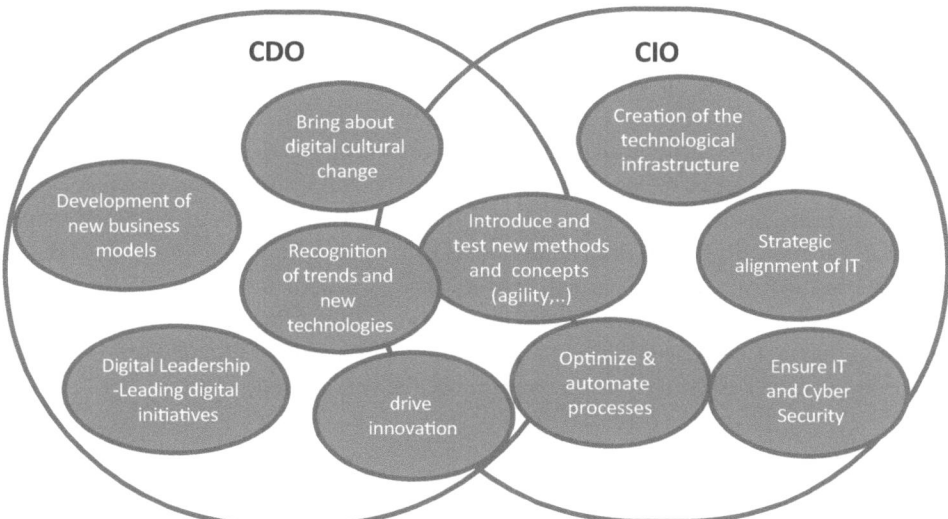

Fig. 6.2 CDO versus CIO: overview of tasks and requirements

- CDOs are responsible for defining and implementing digital trends, new business models, and company-wide strategy changes.
- CDOs are responsible for active demand management. They conduct feasibility and trend/market analyses and propose new requirements to the specialist departments.
- CDOs continually evolve the enterprise architecture.
- CDOs create transformation plans, monitor their implementation, and intervene when necessary.
- CDOs coordinate the digital executives from the individual departments.
- CDOs interface with the chief information officer, chief finance officer, chief operating officer, and chief execution officer.

A typical profile can also be derived from this range of tasks:

- CDOs have successfully completed a degree in business informatics, business administration, engineering, or a comparable field.
- CDOs draw on several years of professional experience in development and innovation management – including leadership experience.
- CDOs have the ability to think together business considerations with technological opportunities, combining an awareness of innovation with realistic assessments.
- CDOs have experience in project management and change management as well as in leading teams – ideally in a transformation context.
- CDOs have excellent communication and negotiation skills and are able to push through their ideas.

In contrast to the CIO's range of tasks, the CDO's is more market and customer oriented. The big question is how CIO and CDO ideally work side by side or together, or which of the two takes on which role and how he thus differentiates himself from the other role.

Both roles must expect that they will change organically in the company according to tasks. Simply because of the open system of the individual teams exchanging and agilely taking on tasks in the company, delegating them, and solving them differently, such changes automatically result. Both areas, the CDO's and the CIO's, will no longer react in a requirements-driven manner but will actively shape – always in relation to success, performance, and profit orientation. Smaller companies will not be able to afford both positions and may not even need them. Here, the CIO will in all likelihood "step up" to the CDO. Because he has the technical prerequisites, the soft skills he acquires.

References

1. AXELOS/TSO (The Stationery Office): "ITIL Foundation, ITIL v4", 1. Auflage, AXELOS/TSO 2019.
2. *Wikipedia*: "Chief Information Officer", https://de.wikipedia.org/wiki/Chief_Information_Officer, abgerufen am 12.02.2020.
3. *Spiegelhoff, Andrea*: "5 Aufgaben für IT-Transformation", Computerwoche, 28.03.2019.

Part IV

Management of IT Organizations

Leadership Principles for CIOs and IT Managers

7

Abstract

Four factors form the foundation of successful management of an IT organization. These include a focus on results, knowledge of the special challenges of managing specialists, concentration on the essentials, and employee development. These four success factors of a modern CIO are presented in detail below.

7.1 Results Orientation and Business Impact as CIO

The image of the IT department and thus also of the CIO as a leader is not always viewed positively by some in the company. Everything always takes far too long to be ready, and something always does not work the way the user would like it to. The whole world is talking about digitalization, but IT is not delivering. That is why many companies have set up their own digital departments, hire a CDO, and develop their own apps. In the worst case, these apps do not even fit into the existing system landscape and cannot be operated internally at all. That does not really make the situation any better. Therefore, the crucial question is: How can IT and the CIO finally show that IT is important and can also deliver?

Unfortunately, IT and its management team often think only input-oriented and pay too little attention to the output. But what counts in the company is the output! You can see this exemplarily in the CVs and conversations with CIOs. There are many remarkable positions and exciting projects listed. But what is often missing is the result: What was really achieved? What were the measurable improvements for the company?

Because only clear added value for the company counts: What benefit have I created and what is better afterward than before?

Examples may include:

- Time-to-market in sales improved by 40%.
- Increase in the degree of automation: Production line x creates a 30% higher output thanks to new software. This means that the production line can produce significantly more and is utilized more efficiently and the contribution margin per product increases by 20%! This has a direct impact on the EBIT and the margin of the company, as this increases by 0.8%.

Real results orientation is always backed up with hard facts. This means for the first example mentioned above, time-to-market increased by 40%, i.e., concretely: When a request on the topic of sales/CRM is received, it now only takes 6 days on average until the function is ready, whereas previously, it was always more than 10 days.

It is always about business impact: Every activity in IT must have an impact on improving the profitability of the company. And this does not mean that you have to work a lot of overtime, work disproportionately hard, and have a lot of stress in an input-oriented way. It is about efficiency in achieving results, first and foremost. For that matter, it does not matter how long it takes to achieve a result. It is irrelevant for the company, for the result, and for the boss whether it takes 3 days to achieve a result or 30 days with 4 h of overtime every day and weekend work. On the contrary, the more efficiently the goal and result are achieved, the better it is for the company and less stressful for the employees.

Goal-oriented work should therefore not be equated with a lot of effort, but with a decisive focus on the desired results. If the SAP implementation in a small plant can be accomplished in 3 weeks, why should one plan in theoretical Gantt diagrams for 3 weeks beforehand and allow 3 months for it?

It is advisable to consider what is necessary to actually achieve the goal and to keep the desired result in mind from the very beginning: What will improve when SAP is implemented in the plant? What are the three points and how can I achieve them as quickly and efficiently as possible? It is always important to remember that it is the result alone that counts and not how you got there or how elegantly and with what impressive project management methods and SCRUM this was realized.

This is pure results orientation and beneficial in the sense of a company.

IT in particular has the task of automating processes and thus making the company more efficient. This higher efficiency often opens up new savings potential. A side effect of these savings is sometimes also the loss of jobs because activities have been automated and no longer have to be performed by people. If, for example, a process is automated to such an extent by new software that three full-time employees are no longer needed, but only half a person, then the question arises as to what should happen with the 2.5 FTEs.

Especially in these situations, it becomes clear that the work as a manager in IT is not always fun and can be fun. The postulate of many politicians, sometimes even managers or company leaders, that work should always be fun and enjoyable is called into question by such situations. Of course, it is nice to have more joyful moments at work, but this cannot be the case all the time. There are always tasks that simply have to be done, and unfortunately, there are also things that do not trigger enthusiasm, such as giving notice. Especially in IT, it often happens that you have to be blamed for system failures, unresolved tickets, or banalities like "the beamer doesn't work! It's IT's fault." Working in IT, especially as a manager, sometimes puts your equanimity to the test.

However, when you focus on the joy of results, it lifts your spirits and makes work fun again. CIOs and IT managers are encouraged to create the conditions for their employees to effectively and successfully achieve results. This can create pride in the things that have been achieved (even if it has not always been easy).

7.2   Managing IT Specialists

Our companies, and especially our highly structured industry, need specialists and expertise. Without real specialists, it would not be possible to create the added value that we do today.

Especially in the IT department of a company, such specialists can be found – sometimes rather pejoratively and sometimes also called praisingly and quite proudly called nerds.

To be able to manage an IT organization, you undoubtedly need these specialists for the various programming languages, for the operation of the infrastructure, and also for the IT-specific processes according to ITIL or other, also very specific standards.

If the head of such a department does not want to get lost in the management world as a specialist himself, then he must understand how specialists are managed. On the other hand, the specialist must not only look at his field with a narrow-minded view, but he must have the view "for the whole"!

Let us take an ERP implementation in the production environment as an example: The specialists involved in the project only pay attention to "their" special task in the overall complex, in this case, for example, the setting or customizing of a function for weighing finished parts. This will eventually work wonderfully, but have the specialists involved realized what this function of weighing finished parts is important for the company and its customers, i.e., what it "contributes to the whole"? This weighing function did not exist before, and the sales department always sold by unit quantities in the hope that all finished parts would weigh the same. Now, however, it has turned out that not all finished parts weigh the same and the company has not been able to realize a significant portion of the sales it actually had. With this new function, invoicing can be done exactly according to weight and the turnover increases. If these effects had been known to the specialists, then a report for the statistical evaluation of the weight of the precast parts and their sales development could have been developed at the same time in order to see what effect this would have. That would have been the view "for the whole." Today, attempts are being made to get a better grip on this through end-to-end processes, but it is still often a problem to keep an eye on the "big picture" and the "why."

But in terms of IT, what is the "contribution to the whole" now, and how can the specialist contribute to the whole instead of just looking at his specialty?

The questions that arise here are: What is the role of IT? What contribution does IT make to the success of the company? What contribution can I, as an IT specialist, make to the company's better results?

This is important to understand, because unfortunately, many IT specialists are simply experts either in programming with Java or developing apps. That is important knowledge per se. But the essential question is: "Whether this specialist knowledge meet the requirement in the company?" In other words, how can the app developer add value to the company?

Beyond that, it is not about "I am…" (e.g., app developer, CIO, or ITIL service manager). There, only the title, i.e., the position in the company, is stated. Rather, it is a statement of what he or she actually does. So, "I ensure in this company that …." To stay with the three examples mentioned above, the sentence could be concluded with "I ensure in this company that

- …our customers no longer have to order awkwardly by phone or fax, but can simply order via an app on their smartphone, thus saving time and, above all, ensuring that the order arrives exactly as it was intended" (app developer).
- …through a high-performance and modern IT the company can work efficiently and our customers get the best possible service for their products" (CIO).
- …all users in the company have a stable, always available IT environment to work in and errors are quickly corrected so that everyone can always work efficiently" (ITIL service manager).

To exaggerate: If it is clear to every specialist how he contributes to the big picture through his work, then he basically no longer needs to be guided, because he knows why he is doing it and what he will contribute to and can therefore lead himself.

7.3   Concentration on the Essentials

Especially the CIO or the IT manager has a hard time in this point: Depending on the company, there are often more than seven or eight departments with different requirements to serve, the technology is developing rapidly, and it is more than understandable if you struggle to stay up to date. Digitalization, artificial intelligence, and other topics must be understood and applied. You have to somehow get to grips with the complexity of the system landscape, and then you are also required to be a leader in addition to the complex technology and to promote change topics.

How is one to do justice to this colorful and, above all, large bouquet of challenges? – the danger of getting bogged down is enormous!

One measure is to concentrate on the essentials. This does not mean that three of eight departments are simply ignored and the system landscape is left as it is. Rather, it means not everything at once, but one thing after the other, because the human brain is not capable of managing many different things at the same time. This means that you cannot be successful in all areas at the same time.

Efficiency and effectiveness in the management of IT can only be achieved by concentrating on the essential and just acute problem. This requires discipline, in the narrower sense a lot of self-discipline, because the danger is very big, especially in the rapidly developing IT-Sectors, to chase the next topic and to neglect the actual topic. At times, one could even speak of stubbornness, which is required here in order not to lose concentration.

A major criticism of IT organizations is often that they cannot get anything done and that everything takes far too long. This prejudice can only be countered by focusing on the essentials. It is not due to a lack of knowledge of methods or an understanding of technology that IT projects are often delayed or even fail. In the vast majority of cases, it is simply due to the "too much" of parallel topics and thus a lack of focus on the essentials.

IT managers and executives have the task of recognizing and implementing this. It is about effectiveness and implementation success, which can only be achieved by concentrating on the little and the essential. What or how much is the little? Psychologist George Miller found out in a study that a maximum of seven plus/minus two things can be accomplished per time unit [1].

Those who think that more is possible will quickly discover that their work balance looks excellent, but their result balance will be very miserable. And that is the situation already described, which is often found in IT: There are dozens of projects underway, but none of them is really finished, and most of them are not as successful as planned. The CIO then always finds himself in "multi-front wars" that can never be won.

7.4 Employee Development: Strengthening Strengths!

A manager is responsible for the right deployment of staff. If CIOs or managing directors seek advice from a trusted person, they often hear that the biggest problem is the IT staff. They are not up to date, there are far too many weaknesses in the modern and absolutely necessary agile method skills, and they are all "just" technicians in the sense of nerds with whom you cannot talk "normally" at all.

If you probe deeper in such conversations, the majority of them only ever present the weaknesses of an IT employee: Most of them have no idea about agile methods, there is a lack of good programmers, and the team leaders are also useless.

This is very unfortunate, and it seems that people and especially leaders only ever see people's weaknesses. Many share the leadership experience of first encountering employee mistakes and failures, along the lines of "That one didn't comment on his source code at all again" or "She just never calls back!" Even customers are already incensed and turn directly to the boss! But even if this is the first feedback managers get about employees, it does not help to complain about it and bury your head in the sand.

The way out is basically quite simple: Everyone has strengths!

It is about identifying the strengths – even if it is just one – of each employee. And this must then be used in such a way that it benefits the company to the maximum. Then this strength can grow and develop even better. That is the task of a manager. (Click here for an article on the topic of "Successful management of IT specialists").

A common mistake in this context is hiring legions of coaches to minimize employees' weaknesses. This is not to say that coaching is not effective. On the contrary, anyone who has experienced professional coaching knows and appreciates the success coaching can bring. But what really happens? The employee's weakness can be worked on sustainably in coaching. The IT employee has become better – but in what sense? He has become better in the sense of "less weak." But between "weak" and "strong," there is still a large field, namely, the field of mediocrity. And most of the time, the coached employees end up exactly in this field. Of course: The previous error or malus no longer occurs every day, but only every 3 days. This can quickly be judged as progress. But be careful: this is a fallacy!

As a leader, you should not mourn the weaknesses of employees. Everyone has weaknesses. It is more goal-oriented to look at the strengths and consider how these strengths can be combined with the ideal role profile in IT. The ideal fit between what the employee can do and what he should do is the goal.

It is important, however, that managers do not completely ignore weaknesses. Weaknesses of employees must be known, not in order to eliminate or improve them, but in order not to make the mistake of putting this employee in a position where he has a weakness.

How should we proceed now, i.e., how can weaknesses and strengths be identified and how can an ideal appointment be made?

In his book *Führen – Leisten – Leben (Leading – Performing – Living)*, Malik uses the analogy of a sports coach or trainer. And this example can also apply very well to IT. A trainer looks closely at which sports his protégé is really good at. If he realizes that he is a good sprinter, then this will be his only field of activity. If this is clear, then within this strength, it is necessary to look at where the weaknesses are, so that these can be improved in order to become the best in the strongest discipline. In the case of sprinters, for example, this means constantly practicing the start, because only the best possible start leads to victory. If this works, one takes the remaining weaknesses within the strength and tackles them. So it is about optimizing the essential strength of a person in the sense of "strengthening strengths."

In conclusion, it remains to be said: An IT executive has the task of creating job profiles as needed for the company. On this basis, the employees best suited to their individual strengths can be placed in the right position and promoted. What does not count as a managerial task is the task of changing employees. That would be an intrusion into a person's personality and therefore not legitimate. But this also means: You have to take what you are given and work with it based on strengths and as effectively as possible. No more and no less.

Reference

1. *Malik, Fredmund*: Führen Leisten Leben, 6. Auflage, Campus Verlag, 2006.

Meaning and Purpose as a Management and Control Instrument

8

Abstract

What is the top priority for the successful management of an IT organization? The CIO must be able to convey meaning and purpose. A goal and a clear vision for IT help to achieve this. This chapter describes how to develop such a vision and a corresponding roadmap.

8.1   Developing a Target Picture for IT

People often smile about a vision, and some people still see it like Helmut Schmidt once did: "Whoever has visions should go to the doctor!"

In German companies, work is still very rational. Processes, structures, clear hierarchies, and work instructions still form the framework of work.

Agility, network organizations, and the start-up wave are bringing movement into the tight framework from the industrial age. However, many still resist this and dismiss it as "newfangled gimmickry."

Not everything that is new has to be good. But on the subject of vision, or today also often called purpose, a clear position should be taken here. If you have been able to experience for yourself in a few projects the power that comes from a jointly supported vision, you will experience your work as meaningful again. For years, studies have been telling us that more than half of internal employees have resigned internally. Could it be because they have lost the meaning of their work?

From there: What is the function of a vision or what should it bring?

- The vision is the foundation and basis for the strategy.

- It provides orientation for one's own actions.
- Visions are runways for goals!
- A vision that is clear and backed up with facts, that creates added value and benefits, and that everyone stands behind arouses conviction and, above all, motivation for all employees!

Admittedly: Many visions – especially those of large corporations – often come across as wooden and somehow all seem the same. How is identification supposed to take place? Why should you, as one of the thousands of employees, like it? But should you quit immediately because of it?

Corporate groups do not have it easy either. For an IT organization with between 20 and 500 employees, it is easier to formulate an IT vision that fits the entire IT and the company.

The following questions are the primary focus on the way to this vision:

- Why do we exist as IT in the company?
- What drives us?
- Where do we want to be in 3 or 5 years?

Vision is developed by going on a journey through time. This may sound strange at first, but that is what vision is all about. You are allowed to dream while you work!

Which events are different from today and with which consequences can be experienced? Pictures are more important than numbers! The managers should have already been there in perspective and emotionally, where they want to get to in reality.

It has proven successful to develop the vision together with the IT management team as well as the management. This means that about five to ten people are involved.

A neutral person can act as moderator, but the CIO can also do this himself, in which case the neutrality is questioned.

The first thing to do is to set a target date. A period of at least 3–4 years and a maximum of 7–8 years in the future is suitable. Five years often form the golden mean, and so here January 1, 2025, is assumed as the target date.

In order to develop this vision or the so-called target image, the following questions and actions will help:

- Each of the participants now puts himself in the year 2025.
- You look at what is happening.
- Which topics are being worked on? What are important projects?
- What are we proud of in the year 2025? What has been achieved together?
- What is all there already and what can you build on?
- How does that feel?

It is now important to write down all these findings in prose; a white sheet of paper that you fill on a full page is perfectly adequate. The facilitator collects these works as an

HOW TO? Examples of good and bad IT target images

☺	☹
"We are evolving as IT to partner with the business at eye level and drive innovation in IoT for production This enables our products to be transported to customers faster and more cost effectively. "	"We deliver the most innovative specialty - solutions in our SAP".
"IT will be an integral part of the business in 2025, helping to develop products for customers and ensuring we remain the market leader in xy through kI innovation in sales."	"We provide satisfaction for our users with state-of-the-art IT!"

Fig. 8.1 Example of good and bad IT target images/IT visions

objective and neutral expert for the strategy work. It is quite possible to create two or three versions of the vision or the target picture. Now each participant is sent all the documents with the request to evaluate them:

• What is good? What is bad? What is missing?

Then comes the workshop, in which the goal is to create an overall vision or an overall goal from all the individual documents. For this purpose, all participants meet to create an overall document and an overall vision from the known individual documents. Ideally, the overall document should be created "live" in a Word document for all to see, so that everyone goes home with the same result in front of them.

Finally, Fig. 8.1 shows examples of successful and less successful target images to provide orientation.

8.2   How Is the IT Target Image Achieved? – Creating the IT Roadmap

Now the path can be developed from the initial situation that exists today to the IT vision that has just emerged.

It is very important not to think from today to the IT vision in 2025, but backward.

That means specifically:

The IT Road map at a glance

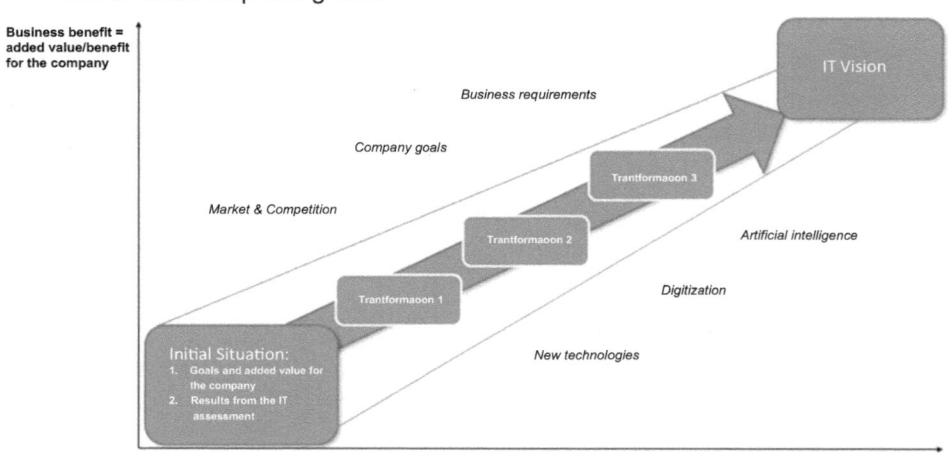

Fig. 8.2 The IT roadmap at a glance

- One is transported back to the year in which one's own target image was concretized as an IT vision!
- What can be seen there? What has been achieved?
- What were the first concrete steps taken at that time?
- What measures were derived?
- What difficulties have been encountered?
- How were these mastered?
- So what does it take to even get there today?

This is the so-called work on the "strategic gap." This strategic gap refers to the area that lies between what is seen in the vision statement and what actually is today. Put another way, "What is the gap between the vision and today's actual state?" (Fig. 8.2).

The IT roadmap provides an overview of all important topics, tasks, and projects for the next 2–3 years on a timeline. The general structure follows the strategy work from phase 3. The starting point of the IT roadmap is the IT assessment with its results and gaps or deltas. The goal of the IT roadmap is the IT vision, in which the gaps and deltas have been resolved to the greatest possible extent through several transformation steps. The IT roadmap thus forms a binding framework that combines the results of the IT assessment and the IT vision with the necessary transformation steps.

To bring these transformation steps to life, a development plan can be placed on top of them. The steps of the transformation are then given contour and are "built on" in annual slices with concrete IT projects.

This makes it very quickly clear what will be "delivered" on the IT roadmap in the coming years and how that will play into the company's IT vision.

Agility and Dynamism Need a New Form of Leadership

9

Abstract

What are the special features of leadership in times of agility and dynamism? What does this mean for the CIO, and what development steps can and must he take in order to lead successfully in a dynamic and agile environment? To this end, this chapter provides a deep insight into the topic of "leadership agility."

9.1 Leadership Agility: Effective Leadership in an Agile and Dynamic World

9.1.1 The Starting Point of Leadership Agility

The book *Leadership Agility* by Bill Joiner [1] already got to the heart of the matter in 2006: The post-industrial era with almost complete interconnectedness through the Internet and the resulting sharp increase in complexity requires a different kind of leadership. Digitalization in all its facets, from Industry 4.0 to IoT to artificial intelligence (AI), touches the core of collaboration, leadership, and control in organizations.

Figure 9.1 illustrates the historical development of dynamics and complexity and shows which leadership models were in the foreground in each case. Starting with the industrial revolution and assembly line work according to Taylorist principles around 1920, complexity and dynamics (i.e., the pace of change) continued to increase. At this time of Taylorism, a company could be run like a relatively simple machine. Employees could be considered parts of that machine. In order for this to function smoothly, they were required to surrender human abilities such as intelligence, imagination, and initiative at the work gate.

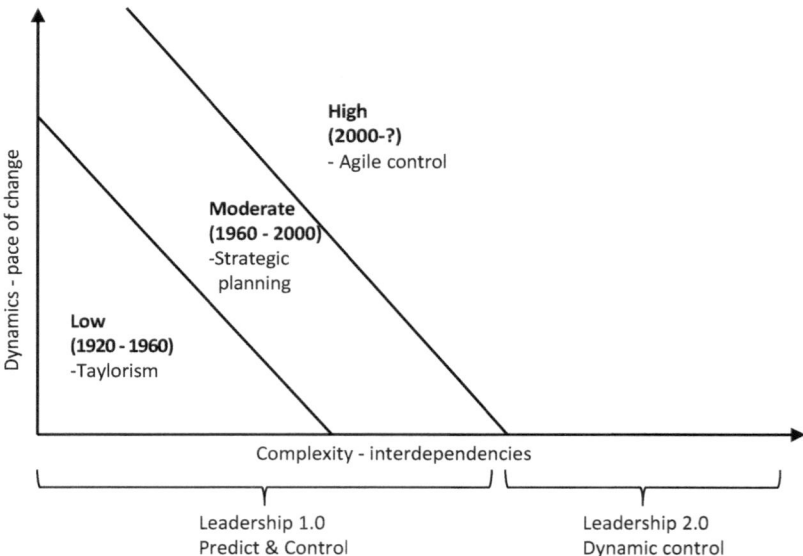

Dynamics - pace of change

High
(2000-?)
- Agile control

Moderate
(1960 - 2000)
-Strategic
planning

Low
(1920 - 1960)
-Taylorism

Complexity - interdependencies

Leadership 1.0   Leadership 2.0
Predict & Control   Dynamic control

Fig. 9.1 The historical development of complexity and dynamics

In the second half of the last century, complexity and dynamics increased significantly. This could be effectively managed through strategic planning. It was the heyday of classical strategy consultancies, which successfully viewed the enterprise as a now much more complicated machine [2]. This machine could be disassembled and analyzed in the context of the market environment and reassembled in a better, more effective way. This approach evolved to a high degree of maturity over the past century. It was wildly successful and enabled huge gains in productivity. At the management level, "Predict and Control" in the sense of setting goals and trying to achieve them was the definitive tool. This management by objectives (MbO) works less and less in today's world and leads to frustration. But how should we manage and lead and how can goals be achieved today?

A variety of evidence is emerging today as to why management by objectives, as well as the old doctrine of strategic planning, is reaching its limits [3]:

• The organization overheats: more and more work is done without any noticeable improvement in results.
• Problems or conflicts that were already thought to have been solved keep resurfacing. Attempts to solve them create new difficulties elsewhere.
• Instead of reflectively creating something new, the reaction is reflexive – either with actionism or spreading paralysis.
• The control and reporting system (i.e., the old control approaches) are being tightened in an attempt to get a grip on what is becoming increasingly difficult to control.
• Burnout is on the rise.

These are clear signs that the governance model itself has reached its limits in terms of thinking, action, and effectiveness.

In particular, the IT department and its managers are affected by this change at its core. In IT, the dynamics and complexity are particularly high due to the ever faster advancing technologization (see Moore's law). In order not to be driven by constant innovations at this level, the CIO must become an innovation driver.

9.1.2 How to Become an Innovation Driver?

First of all, it is important to know that it is, so to speak, inherent in innovations that they almost never take place in a strategy-driven, top-down manner. Innovations cannot be "decreed" by strategy meeting but simply take place in many places in the company at the same time. But only if certain conditions are met. These include, for example, a high degree of self-responsibility among employees, personal initiative, and things like job rotation and job enlargement. Tensions and problems are responded to immediately, and the information they contain is used as creative potential. In addition, hierarchies have become very flat or have been replaced by network-like structures.

In the very readable book *Reinventing Organizations* by Frederic Laloux [3], examples of such organizations can be found. Using 12 companies as examples, it shows how self-organization takes place and what effects it has on the employees themselves but also on the competitiveness of the company.

Agilely managed companies are significantly more successful economically than companies with more rigid structures and processes. This is why we see initiatives such as self-directing teams or agile project management in many places, even in conventionally managed organizations, which are also intended to make the IT organization more agile. So why is it that some of these experiments release a lot of energy and solve issues that previously seemed unsolvable, while others tend to cause frustration and disappointment after sometimes only a short time and turn "agile" into a modern management misnomer?

Often it is simply due to two things:

1. People are under the misconception that agility does not require leadership.
2. You simply copy procedures and models without understanding them.

Regarding point 1, agile initiatives can only be successful if they are designed by people who bring an agile leadership mindset.

Agile leadership not only requires a new set of competencies and methods but also an attitude that is diametrically opposed to classic management and control thinking in many places.

In order to lead agile projects to success, you need not only a set of methods but above all a very specific mindset. If this is missing, failure is often pre-programmed.

For example, Laloux [3] in his study of agile organizations concluded that it is precisely this agile leadership mindset that is needed to shape an agile organization.

This leads to the question of what exactly an "agile leadership attitude" is and how it differs from the classic understanding of leadership.

9.1.3 Leadership Agility: From Conventional Leadership to Agile Leadership

In the course of many research projects, it has been shown that managers develop through different, describable levels of leadership agility as their leadership personality matures and that these levels differ fundamentally in their attitudes and understanding of leadership. Not only characteristic observable leadership behavior but also the mental-emotional capacities underlying this behavior have been studied.

Figure 9.2 shows in which areas of complexity and dynamics the three most important levels in the leadership context show their greatest effectiveness – from the tactical-problem-solving-oriented "Expert" to the strategic-goal-oriented "Achiever" (both variants of conventional leadership) to the visionary-development-oriented "Catalyst" (agile leadership).

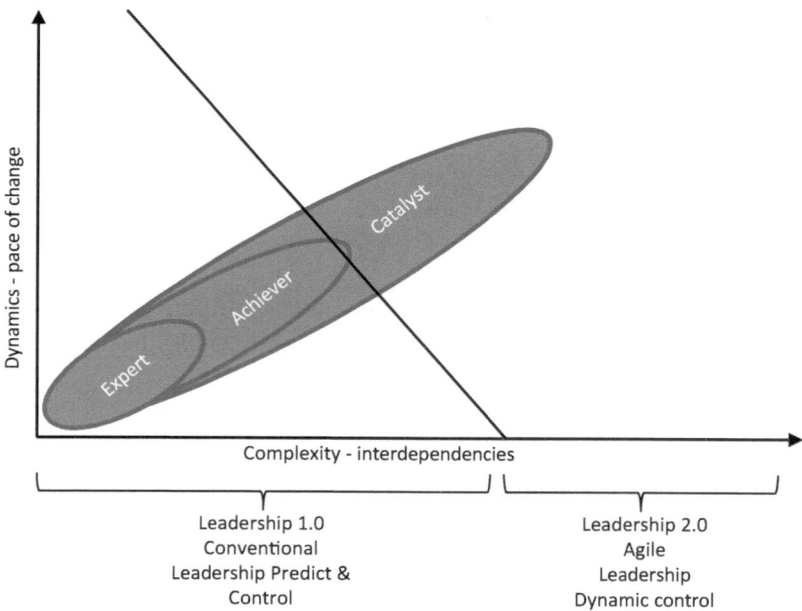

Fig. 9.2 The management levels in the context of dynamics and complexity

The Expert: "I Know It"

When complexity and dynamics are manageable, it is possible to lead as the one who knows how. Managers at the expert level see their professional competence as the basis of their authority as a leader. Therefore, they attach great importance to being up to date in their field in order to be able to give well-founded instructions to their employees. Expert management is strong in bringing known topics into operational implementation. At the same time, there is a strong desire to solve problems by means of their own experience.

At the same time, this is the home of micromanagement, often combined with the burden of a heavy workload. The view is tactical-operational and is primarily directed at one's own area of responsibility. The focus is currently on one problem, one person, one function, with little regard for cross-functional dependencies.

The Achiever: "I Know the Target"

While an Expert leader manages tasks, the Achiever manager sees his job as leading people. He is concerned with setting a whole system in motion toward strategic goals and motivating others through satisfying collaboration toward a challenging goal. The focus is strategic with the customer in mind, whether internal or external. Goals and results play a central role. He relies heavily on employees with a similar "mindset" who are quickly identified as high performers. He gives them freedom in their implementation. An Achiever manager has a clear view of the entire functional system and thus a good overview of the stakeholders who are important for achieving his goals. He sees teamwork as the key to success. Thus, in regular team meetings, he will ensure that there is exchange and debate on issues that are important to him.

The Catalyst: "I Shape Effective Collaboration"

If the Achiever manager's focus is on achieving strategic goals, the Catalyst leader's vision extends beyond that. He realizes that the answer to increasing uncertainty lies in an agile organizational culture. In martial arts, there is a technique of aiming through the target to the target behind the target. By analogy, he will try to shape the path to strategic goals in a way that fosters the creation of an agile and participatory high-performance culture, characterized by values such as transparency, personal responsibility, openness, and equal footing. In doing so, he thinks of the organization and its issues not only as a functional organism but also as a complex social system with a high awareness of the human and emotional issues involved.

The IT director of a fast-growing Internet start-up once put it this way: "I used to be an architect of IT systems. Today, I'm an architect of a social system."

Figure 9.3 illustrates the difference between conventional and agile leadership. The left box shows conventional leadership. The primary focus is on achieving goals through direct leadership from manager to employee. This is done through instruction, target agreement, or delegation.

In contrast, the manager in the figure on the right is no longer shown in the box, but instead depicts it as a kind of framework for action. The employees are closely networked

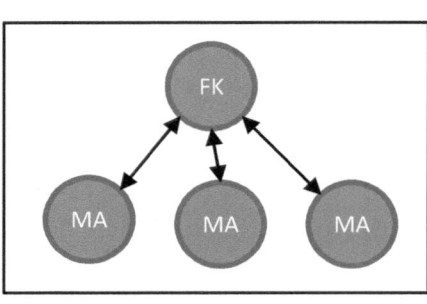
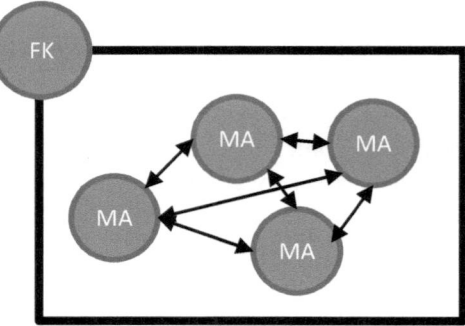

Conventional Leadership
Predict & Control

Agile leadership
Dynamic control

Fig. 9.3 Conventional versus agile leadership

with each other. This means that this form of organization can respond quickly to as yet unknown developments. Also, there is no direct link between the leader and the employees, because leadership here does not function on the basis of direct instruction and control, but the leader sets the framework. This framework can become clear through the following questions:

- Who are we? What do we stand for? What are our guiding principles?
- What is our orientation? Where do we want to develop?
- What are goals and objectives that we need to achieve?
- How can we best use our individual talents to achieve this?
- What are the framework conditions and guard rails of our actions?

Within this framework, space is created for effective self-organization and individual potential development. The cohesion of the company is therefore no longer primarily ensured by central control but by a common understanding of strategic orientation and principles guiding action.

Cultural transformation starts with me.

A Catalyst leader knows that culture starts with him. Therefore, he will not delegate culture development to HR but will start in his own management team and use it as a kind of laboratory in which his target culture is lived and radiates into the organization.

Table 9.1 shows the differences between Expert, Achiever, and Catalyst leadership. It is important to understand that the next higher level includes the previous one(s). In other words, the Achiever can always draw on the elements learned as an Expert. Likewise, the Catalyst can draw on both Achiever and Expert experience and use it as needed.

Following [3].

So what is the core of Catalyst leadership and what underlies it?

Table 9.1 The difference between Expert, Achiever, and Catalyst

	Conventional management		Agile leadership
	Expert	Achiever	Catalyst
Focus	Tactical and problem-solving oriented. The basis of leadership is professional authority	Strategic and results-oriented. Leadership mobilizes for goal achievement	Visionary, potential, and development oriented. Leadership inspires and empowers
Think and act	Looking at individual topics. Thinking in terms of professional logic	View of the functional system. Goal-oriented, rational, analytical, focus on the factual level (numbers, data, facts)	View of the functional and social system. Conscious design of the interaction of people to achieve common goals
Conflict management	Right and wrong, winning and losing	Compromise/deal	Conflict as creative potential, search for win-win solutions
Talk and listen	Communication of the "right" idea	Discussion, competition of defined ideas	Creative activity for the further development of ideas
Leadership style	Focus where it burns, focus on main topics	Involve and delegate more than solve yourself	Design of self-developing processes
Control model	Company as a complicated machine "predict and control": Efficient implementation of known goals	Company as a complicated machine "predict and control": Efficient implementation of known goals	Company and market as complex systems of agile control: Quick responses to unknown developments
Values	Predictability, clarity, unambiguity, facts	Performance, efficiency, measurability, growth, competition, result	Learning, development, potential development, perspective integration, flexibility, creativity, balance, meaning
Distribution in %	55	35	10

- The ability to combine different even apparently contradictory perspectives into an overall view and to make decisions on the basis of this overall view.
- Quickly adopting an "eagle's eye view" to bring together complex problems at this level and enable entirely new decisions to be made.
- Mindfulness as a continuous (so to speak "online") capacity of reflection: a perceptive distance to one's own view of things and the source of one's own thinking, feeling, and acting.
- Change of perspective: the ability to detach oneself from one's own point of view to such an extent that it becomes possible to take an authentic interest in a completely different point of view.

- This attitude is the basis for multi-perspective thinking: the ability to perceive different even very contradictory views of a situation, a topic, or a problem at the same time and to bring them together again on a higher level.
- In addition, a calm approach to one's own fears and weaknesses is an absolute prerequisite for embodying these abilities in a stable manner, not only in fair weather but also in unavoidable crises.

These competencies are a prerequisite for designing agile structures and processes, creating the necessary space for them and maintaining them even under pressure.

9.1.4   How Can Agile Leadership Be Implemented in the IT Organization?

First of all, the following remains to be said from the previous findings of the concept of "leadership agility":

- In many companies and IT organizations, conventional management according to Predict and Control and strategic planning and management according to goals are increasingly reaching their limits.
- Agile leadership has not yet established itself as a healing alternative method and is often understood as a "template" or process model and thus not properly introduced.
- In this respect, agile control differs radically from conventional control.
- The most important building block for success: Agile initiatives need leadership, but no longer at Expert or Achiever level, but at Catalyst level.

▶   **Important** Agile structures do not require less leadership, but rather a completely different kind of leadership. The Catalyst embodies the prototype of the agile understanding of leadership. It is clear that agile organizations can only be successfully introduced and lived by the appropriate leadership mindset. From this perspective, the following questions arise for IT leadership and personnel development:

- How can the CIO and senior management become sponsors of agile initiatives?
- Where in an IT organization is the highest need for more agility?
- How do you identify decision-makers or leaders who are capable of driving agile initiatives?
- What needs to be done to get these people into the right places?
- How do you create the freedom that enables these pioneers as catalysts to develop new structures and processes?

- How can HR development help to identify and develop such Catalyst leaders?
- How are individuals with Catalyst potential recruited?

It can be helpful here to identify innovators with catalyst potential, to promote them with the help of targeted development programs, and to network them with one another, for example, by having them work together on significant change projects. A positive side effect is that this helps to retain high-potential employees.

Moreover, companies and their IT organizations, where expert-achiever leadership has been the norm for decades, face the historic challenge of moving a sufficient number of managers to a whole new level of leadership.

Traditional leadership development offers a variety of proven and powerful tools to support the developmental step from the tactical-operational Expert level to the strategic-goal-oriented Achiever level. These classic leadership competencies create the basis for agile leadership.

Agile leadership, however, requires a holistic rethinking of leadership. It is based on an attitude that is radically different from previous images of leadership. The development of a new attitude does not happen through cognitive insight alone, but above all through profound personal experience. Development programs aimed at agile leadership therefore need a high proportion of self-reflection and experience-based personal development. Transformative coaching can also be a crucial catalyst in this transition.

9.2   Specifics of Leadership in the Digital Age

The digital transformation already has the keyword in it: change. It is therefore a process of change. This change takes place on many levels: strategy, processes, culture, and also leadership.

What is the most important thing in such change processes, especially in terms of good leadership in the digital transformation?

- Openness.
- Honesty.
- Authenticity.

In addition, digital issues also play a role, such as:

- Openness for new things – awakening the spirit of innovation.
- Mastering and reducing complexity.
- Understanding and being able to adapt new technologies.

In addition, there is an essential point – challenging and promoting employees – because it's about lifelong learning. It's about being able to understand, anticipate, and then master new challenges again and again, because digitization is not a fad that will be replaced by something else the day after tomorrow.

Especially when it comes to promotion and lifelong learning, it is very important to really take everyone in the company along on the journey: both the baby boomer generation and the digital natives (see also Part I of this leadership 4.0 series on the topic of the generations growing together in the digital company).

Another point about leadership in the digital age revolves around processes. Instead of the internal focus on optimizing the company through more efficient processes, the focus in the digital world is finally back on the customer. The keyword is customer centricity.

Last but certainly not least is the topic of "strategy and vision." The manager must be able to exemplify the digital strategy and vision and fill it with life again and again.

With all the aspects that have been mentioned here, one thing always applies as a matter of course: The manager sets a good example. This is the only way to ensure authenticity.

In summary, the following points emerge:

1. Openness to new things – awakening the spirit of innovation.
2. Mastering and reducing complexity.
3. Understanding and being able to adapt new technologies.
4. Challenging and promoting employees – lifelong learning/knowledge management.
5. Customer centricity instead of internal process optimization.
6. Speed.
7. Strategy and vision as a foundation.

References

1. *Joiner, Bill & Josephs, Steven*: "Leadership Agility: Five Levels of Mastery for Anticipating and Initiating Change", 2. Auflage, Jossey-Bass. 2006.
2. *Brenner, W./Witte, C.*: "Erfolgsrezepte für CIOs", 1. Auflage, Hanser, 2007.
3. *Küster, Hermann*: "Leadership Agility – die Führungsherausforderung in der IT" erschienen in Michael Lang: "CIO 3.0: Die neue Rolle des IT Managers", Symposium Publishing 2014.

Abstract

In the past, management by objective (MbO) – i.e., leading by setting clear objectives
and controlling the objectives – was modern management. This has become completely
obsolete. The new motto is management by OKRs as known from Google. In the following chapter, you will learn what this is all about.

10.1 Definition and Objectives of OKRs

Google is often called the pioneer and inventor of OKRs (Objectives and Key Results) and
has been using this method since the early 2000s. For a few years now, the OKRs method
has also gained acceptance among German start-ups and is just now finding its way into
traditional companies.

Simply put, behind the OKRs is a leadership model based on goals.

At first glance, one might think that this is nothing really new, since target agreements
and management by objectives (MbO) have been common practice in corporate groups for
many years.

The advantage of OKRs over the previous target agreements lies in the following points:

- OKRs link strategy/vision directly to small team goals.
- In this context, the objectives are set "in the long term," i.e., a maximum of 3–6 months
  in the future, in contrast to the strategy, which is set for the very long term (3–5 years),
  and also in contrast to the target agreements, which usually cover 1 year.

- The objectives must always be in line with the strategy, i.e., on the way to the strategy, they must be the currently appropriate objectives that further pave the way to the strategy.
- OKRs thus create clarity about the tasks to be completed in the short term within the company and ensure transparency.
- The key here is that the emotional attachment to a short-term goal is maintained over the 3 months and thus the motivation to achieve it is great. In the pure pursuit of a strategy with a long-term horizon, one quickly runs out of breath, and the strategy process stalls or is aborted.

The "O" of OKRs stands for "Objectives" (=goals; "WHY are we doing this?") and the "KR" for "Key Results" (=result criteria; "HOW do we achieve the goal?"). To keep these objectives and results feasible and realistic, there may be a maximum of five Objectives and four Key Results. Less is often more: three Objectives with, e.g., a maximum of three Key Results per Objective are often sufficient (Fig. 10.1).

The goals must always contribute to the strategy and should be defined both top-down (by the management or the board) and bottom-up (by the employee or team). The 40–60 rule has established itself as a sensible mix, i.e., 40% of the goals come from management and 60% of the goals come from the operational level. This promotes responsibility and emotional attachment for the goals and objectives among all employees.

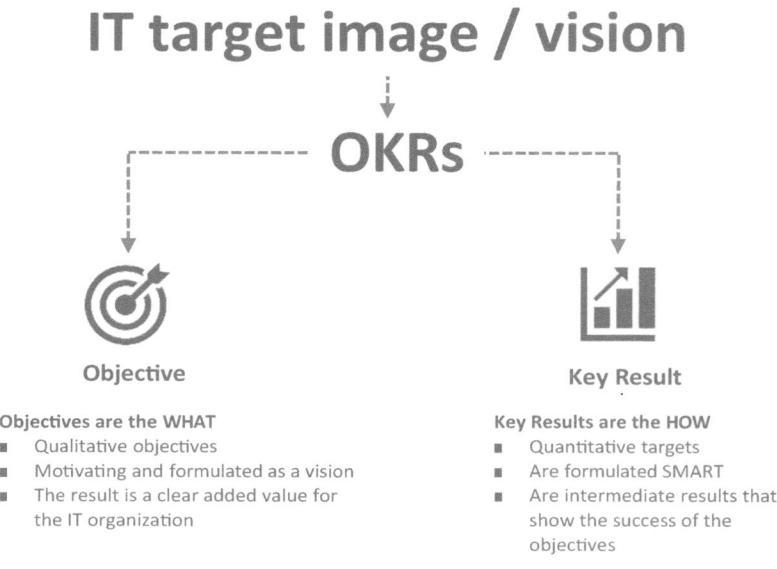

IT target image / vision

OKRs

Objective

Key Result

Objectives are the WHAT
- Qualitative objectives
- Motivating and formulated as a vision
- The result is a clear added value for the IT organization

Key Results are the HOW
- Quantitative targets
- Are formulated SMART
- Are intermediate results that show the success of the objectives

Fig. 10.1 OKR: an overview

10.2   Procedure for the Preparation of OKRs for IT

This determination and definition of goals or objectives takes place quarterly, i.e., every 3 months. In addition, three essential meetings have emerged as useful for the effective management of OKRs:

- Weeklies: These are weekly meetings at which all those involved discuss the progress made with a view to achieving the objectives and adjust the action planning in line with requirements.
- Reviews: Here, the objectives, the key results, and any obstacles encountered are discussed with each other. In general, there is always a backlog and a list of "things we are not doing," which are always used in this review.
- Retros: In this meeting, the OKRs process as such is scrutinized by all participants with the aim of drawing conclusions on future possibilities for improvement.

What is important in the definition of OKRs?
The following things must be adhered to in the Objectives:

- Objectives must answer the question of "WHY" and not "WHAT."
- An objective must be formulated in such a way that it describes a state in the future.
- Objectives are qualitative in nature, i.e., not numbers or percentages, but the benefits and added value to be achieved.
- Objectives must always be ambitious and should ideally feel uncomfortable and challenging.

The following things should be noted for the key results:

- The key results as result criteria describe the "HOW," e.g., with the sentence structure "…in which…."
- Key Results are always measurable, i.e., use ZDF (numbers, data, facts).
- Relevance is important: Does my Key Result contribute to the Objective in the sense of "Which Core Results really make the Objective happen?"

A small example of OKRs:

Vision: "We build cars in which no one dies anymore!"

Strategy in the sense of a strategic goal: "Thanks to the latest software and forecasting technology, our cars can foresee all traffic obstacles, assess them correctly and thus react very early and avoid accidents."

Based on this long-term strategy, the first OKRs are now defined on a 3-month basis, the so-called first OKRs period:

Objective: "A first roadmap and conceptual designs for the development of the required software and forecasting technology have been developed."

Key Result: "Research identified the most advanced 10 AI software tools in terms of traffic analytics."

Key Result: "Validation of 5 current radar and sensor modules in terms of suitability for vision."

Key Result: "5 ideas emerged for redesigning the car in line with the vision."

Cascading of the OKRs to the areas (here exemplarily two areas):

Objective for the IT department: "To achieve the strategy, IT is building AI expertise and machine learning know-how."

Key Result: "A skills matrix has been created for all IT staff to analyze AI skills including fit/gap analysis."

Key Result: "7 companies have been identified in the market that help build AI expertise or have AI software that can be adapted internally."

Objective for technical development (TE): "Search for a radar solution on the market that meets the requirements of the strategy."

Key Result: The requirements for a high-precision radar are specified in 80% detail.

Key Result: Five companies specialized in high-precision radar development were identified.

In addition to this example, Fig. 10.2 serves once again to compare the old world with the new. Besides the replacement of targets by OKRs, as this example shows, there are mainly three things that are different and new:

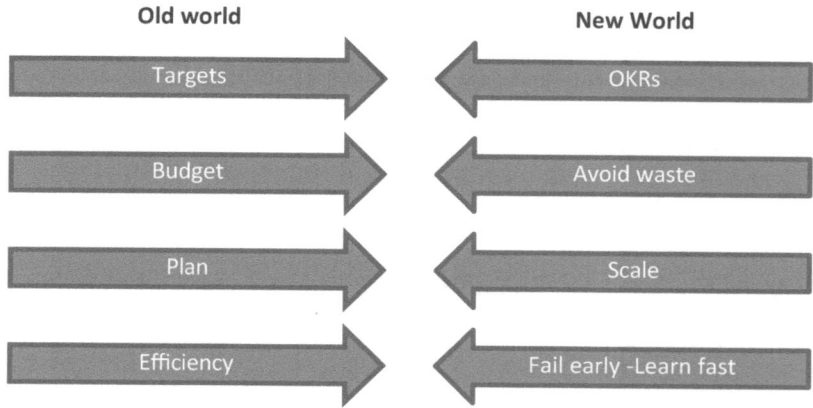

Fig. 10.2 Old world vs. new world (targets vs. OKR)

- Instead of planning via budgets, it's about avoiding waste.
- Instead of putting the plan first and trying to meticulously plan everything ahead, OKRs thinking is about scaling.
- Instead of continuing to turn the efficiency screw, it is more about the principle of "learn fast – fail early." Failure in new learning experiences is allowed, and everything is conceivable.

Leadership and Team Building: The Five Phases According to Tuckman

11

Abstract

Developing a team is one of the essential tasks of the CIO. Tuckman has found that such team development always follows similar patterns and procedures. This is a great help for IT managers to consciously and actively manage the team development process. Here are the five phases of team building in detail.

For IT managers and especially IT project managers, team building and development play a major role. It determines the actual success of a project. The management of IT specialists as so-called knowledge workers was already examined in detail in a previous article. This article now deals with team building in IT projects or in newly formed IT departments.

Excitingly, such team building always follows relatively similar patterns, as the American psychologist Bruce Tuckman already found out in the mid-1960s. The "five phases of team building" named after him show this very clearly and thus provide all team and project leaders with a very helpful guide.

Similar to the change curve, the five phases show very precisely where the team is in its development and what is needed for the development to progress further.

The following are the five phases according to Tuckman as described in Fig. 11.1 and a performance assessment of the team as well as the possible or necessary actions of the manager or team leader:

1. **Forming (The Orientation and Finding Phase)**

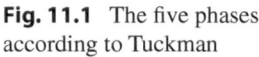

Fig. 11.1 The five phases according to Tuckman

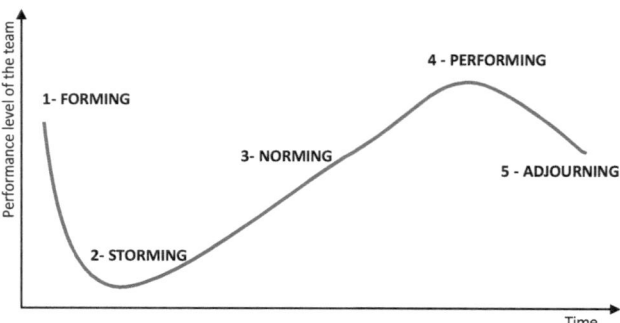

In an IT project, this phase starts with the official kickoff of the project. All project members meet, and the so-called orientation and finding phase ("forming") begins. The individual project or team members get to know each other and try to build up an initial group feeling. This getting to know each other involves uncertainties, and therefore, the mood in this phase is one of cautious restraint. There is still a lack of clarity about the roles and positions of the individual team members. In order to dissolve this ambiguity, for example, it is examined how one should or may behave in this group. Everyone tries to find his own role in the team. On the other hand, the motivation in this first phase is still relatively high for some team members, because they are excited and looking forward to the new task in the group. It is now important that basic structures and rules are found and formulated together.

- *Characteristics*: This phase is often characterized by a rather formal and cautious "feeling out."
- *Performance of the team*: Not very high yet, because goals and rules are not yet clear and the own finding and placing in the team has to be found and is therefore in the foreground.

Task of the team leader

- Provide orientation and a framework: agree on common rules.
- Ensure a pleasant climate so that everyone feels welcome.
- Encourage the process of team members getting to know each other.
- Offering each individual the opportunity to find his or her own place in the team.
- Build trust within the team.
- Active management of the team.

2. **Storming (The Conflict Phase)**

The second phase is defined as the conflict phase or "close combat phase" and is called "storming" according to Tuckman. After the cautious feeling out and getting to know each other in the first phase, the first conflicts now come to light. Typical conflict situations often revolve around the distribution of power, priorities, and objectives. Problem situations can be assigned to two essential types of conflicts, the task conflicts and the role conflicts. In the case of task conflicts, the issue is that a team member does not or cannot complete his or her task in the way that individual group members expect. This quickly leads to very emotional conflicts. In addition to task conflicts, there are also role conflicts during the storming phase. For example, it may turn out that ideas of individual team members are incompatible with reality. At this point, the first attempts are made to define one's own territory. The clash of dominant characters can influence the entire work process of a team.

- *Characteristics of this phase*: From the leadership's point of view, this second phase is difficult and sometimes unpleasant, but it is also the most important phase, because, if the existing conflicts are handled properly in this phase, the team will be able to achieve good results later on.
- *Performance of the team*: Decreases significantly and drops to a low point.

Task of the team leader

- Do not prevent but allow conflicts within the group.
- Proposing ways of dealing with conflict and giving everyone a chance to have their say.
- Here, team leaders have the role of mediator, by defusing conflict potential, and the role of driver, by setting concrete goals and directing the team's focus toward them.
- It is important to create the basis for a successful cooperation of the team. This becomes possible as soon as the individual team members have found their roles and positions.
- Active leadership with a cool head and a lot of empathy.

3. **Norming (The Regulation Phase)**

Phase 3 can be recognized by the fact that the conflicts from phase 2 are resolved and a sense of togetherness develops, so that the team members orient themselves more toward the team than toward themselves. New rules of cooperation emerge, and this is also the defining heading in norming: regulation phase. Ideally, a common goal emerges that takes up the partial goals of the individuals.

Roles and relationships of the individual team members crystallize, and the cooperation becomes closer and closer. As a result, the team can also better dedicate itself to the actual tasks and deliver performance.

The "we" feeling increases strongly. This usually leads to a significantly increased motivation, because everyone wants to contribute to the greater whole and now also knows exactly what their task is.

- *Characteristics of this phase*: The team's communication at this stage is increasingly task-oriented and less relationship-oriented. There are common rules about how to work together.
- *Performance of the team*: Still low at the beginning, but increases significantly.

Task of the team leader

- Moderate.
- Emphasize connecting elements.
- Advise the team on agreeing rules for living together.
- Ensure that targets are met.

4. **Performing (The Performance Phase)**

The fourth phase is the so-called performance phase (performing according to Tuckman), and it lives up to its name: because now the team has reached the highest performance level. This has only become possible through the constructive confrontations in the two previous phases. The team has now become a real team, working for each other and supporting each other. The interaction in the team is accordingly characterized by mutual acceptance, respect, and appreciation. Differences between team members are no longer used for conflicts but are actively used for the optimized implementation of goals, because now it is no longer the performance of the individual that counts, but the achievement of group goals.

- *Characteristics of this phase*: In this phase, the team's results are more than the sum of their parts.
- *Performance of the team*: Increases strongly and settles at a high level.

Task of the team leader

- Leadership of the team rather restrained, focus rather on stakeholders outside the team and its representation toward management.
- Promotion of individual team members (if necessary).
- Repeated reflection and review of team objectives.
- Continue to have confidence in the team.

5. **Adjourning (The Dissolution Phase)**

According to Tuckman, this last phase is particularly important for projects, because every project is a time-limited undertaking with a clear end. This is determined by the fact that the project goals have been achieved. The project members go back to the line and to their daily business. But teams do not exist forever either, and this phase is also very important here in order to complete team goals or at least make them professionally transferable.

An important feature of this breakup phase is that there can often be a reduction in performance some time before the team separates. Infact, some do not want to go back to their old daily business. This causes uncertainty, the motivation in the team or project decreases, and the danger of distraction from the actual goals is relatively high. A lot of tact and, above all, leadership is required here.

But when the goal has been reached, it is time to part with the completed task. Part of the process of parting is, of course, pride in the challenge or task solved by the team. It is important to say goodbye in an appropriate manner and to end the project adequately.

- *Characteristics of this phase*: Uncertainty about the future of individual team members can lead to a loss of motivation and thus pose a threat to the achievement of goals. A lot of leadership skill is required here.
- *Performance of the team*: Decreasing.

Task of the team leader

- Now take active leadership and control again, so that the goals are really achieved and a crowning conclusion can be made.
- Provide feedback and reflection for team members. Identify potential and future perspectives and discuss with line managers.
- Shaping the farewell to the team and each individual.

Finally, it is important to know that the phases can also occur simultaneously and repeatedly. For example, it is possible that parts of a team already know each other from previous projects and therefore arrive relatively quickly at the performing phase. Other team members, however, are still in the forming phase. The same can happen when a new member joins an existing team or when an important member leaves.

If a leader is aware of this fact, he/she can react accordingly in the various possible "phase combinations." For example, if a team member – in contrast to the rest of the team – has not yet reached a certain phase, it may be more helpful to help this person to the next level instead of exerting pressure.

Conclusion: The five phases according to Tuckman make it very clear that as a manager, you have to perform very different tasks for a team or project in order to achieve optimal performance. The phases serve as a mirror and show clearly where one is at the moment and how to act in this phase. It thus turns out to be a very helpful leadership tool that is easy to apply and yet highly effective.

Important Cultural Aspects of an IT Organization

12

Abstract

Leadership and culture belong together. But how do you develop a "good" culture in IT? What can be tools, structures, and systemic features that help the CIO understand where IT stands culturally and how to influence the development of a culture? This chapter will help you to do that.

12.1 Culture and IT

In addition to the hard facts of an IT organization, such as the IT processes and the structural and procedural organization, there are many soft factors. These are generally referred to as culture. These include, for example, the way in which people think, decide, and act in the IT organization and how the IT organization "breathes." The questions are: "What patterns and behaviors are lived in the IT organization? What are our beliefs and what do we orient ourselves to – even unconsciously – when making important decisions?"

The well-known management patron Peter Drucker put it very nicely in a nutshell: "Culture eats Strategy for Breakfast!" This does not mean that strategy is not important. But the seemingly invisible and elusive culture has a major impact on the success of a company and thus also of an IT organization.

Especially when it comes to change, the cultural component is crucial. You could also say: The strategy provides the instructions for action and the implementation, and the "actual living" of this strategy is a process of change. And this process of change has to do with people and their values, norms, behaviors, and beliefs. And it is these things that describe culture. The important thing to understand here is that there is no such thing as a "good" or "bad" culture. Every culture is meaningful and meaningful for the employees in its own way.

In order to make this often somewhat vague and intangible topic of culture tangible, one differentiates between different levels of culture. Edgar Schein is an organizational psychologist from the USA and is considered one of the pioneers in the field of corporate culture. He has developed three levels for a better understanding of the concept of culture, which are shown in Fig. 12.1.

According to Schein, the three levels of culture can be described as follows (adapted from [1]):

- *Level 1*: On the surface are the visible behaviors, such as shared language, history, and rituals. Examples might include: How do IT employees converse with each other? What are the special posters and logos in the office space? What are the most popular software tools and what does not work at all?
- *Level 2*: Below level 1 are the norms and values that belong to the behaviors. This can be reflected, for example, in the way we deal with each other in IT or also in the direction of the specialist departments. Which values are important to us? Is it honesty, for example? Are we rather technology-loving or do we see the world rather conservatively or very optimistically for the future?
- *Level 3*: At the lowest level are the things that are taken for granted for the way one reacts to the environment (the so-called basic assumptions). These basic assumptions are not questioned or discussed. They are so deeply ingrained in thinking that they are not consciously perceived by members of the organization. These include, for example,

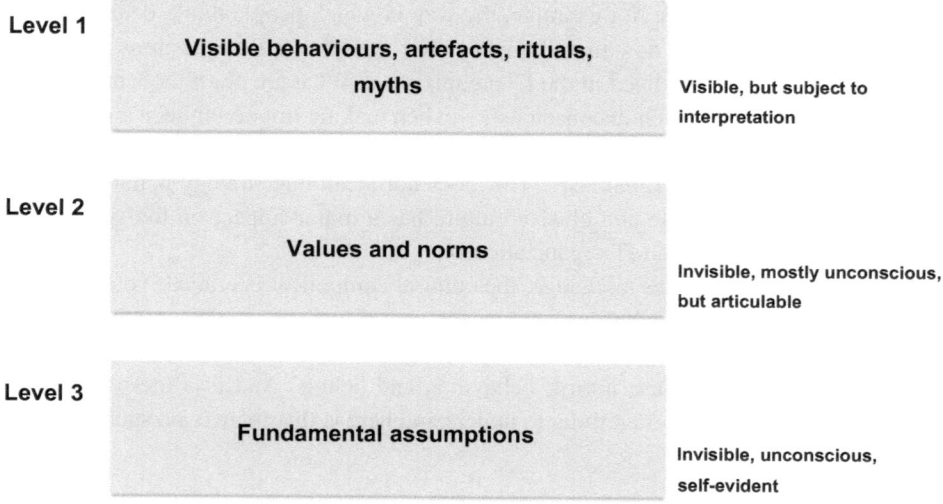

Fig. 12.1 The three levels of culture according to Edgar Schein

beliefs and deep convictions (e.g., "SAP is the best ERP and everything else makes no sense at all!").

The introduction and use of agile methods such as SCRUM in IT projects is a typical example of a major change process in IT. The success of the use of SCRUM is not determined by the correct application of this method but by the interaction with each other and the acceptance and understanding of "Why are we using this?". You succeed on a completely different level, that of culture. Existing beliefs from the times of the waterfall model can be, for example, "Without concrete planning of the whole topic, nothing can come of it!". Such beliefs can quickly lead to rejecting agile methods out of hand. If one has to use them anyway due to specifications by the superior, it will not be successful.

Culture is thus the essential influencing factor and content-related "object" when it comes to changes in IT organizations. In the following, three essential topics are considered in more detail in order to establish a successful culture in IT for the tasks at hand:

- The foundation for a successful IT culture is trust.
- How can the systemic perspective help us to understand culture even better?
- What is special about a culture in the digital age?

12.2   Trust Is the Basis for a Healthy Corporate Culture in IT

Trust is not the only building block of a successful cultural foundation, but it is an essential one. Therefore, with a view to leadership in IT, the question will be raised: "How do you create trust in an IT organization and what does that mean for everyday leadership?"

Many IT managers have learned the hard facts of management and apply them textbook-like in their IT department, theoretically doing everything right. Nevertheless, large implementation projects always succeed only very tenaciously and with a lot of struggle and time investment. What is the reason for this and what is missing?

When you get to the bottom of this question, the topic of trust often comes up. Because if the IT managers have the trust of their employees and on this basis there is a good climate in the team and work is really enjoyable, then things succeed much more easily. Large projects are always transformations, i.e., not changes on a technical level, but above all on a human level. Automation creates new processes and workflows, and these have an enormous impact on people: Activities change or even disappear altogether. Habits have to change and old beliefs are suddenly no longer correct. This shakes the innermost part of the human being.

Only if there is a close relationship of trust and mutual confidence in such situations can such phases be shaped together and successfully.

Malik has set out a few rules for managers that are also very valuable for IT managers when it comes to building trust [2]:

- Mistakes of the employees are also mistakes of the boss.
- The boss's mistakes are the boss's mistakes.
- Employees' successes belong to the employees: As a boss, you don't adorn yourself with other people's feathers.
- Successes of the boss – if he alone should have such – he can claim for himself: Good managers, however, still say "We" have achieved it together.

In conclusion, there are four rules for IT leaders to build and establish trust (adapted from Malik [2]):

1. If you want to create trust, you have to listen.
2. Anyone interested in trust must be genuine.
3. If you want to create trust, you have to have integrity of character.
4. If you want to create trust, you have to get rid of schemers.

12.3 The Systemic View of IT Organizations: Innovation Through IT and Dealing with Uncertainty

The current and upcoming market environment is often outlined with the abbreviation VUCA. This stands for volatility, uncertainty, complexity, and ambiguity (VUCA).

In such a world of high dynamics, complexity, and uncertainty, the traditional, rather mechanistic image of IT with long-term planning, standardized process models, and rigid IT systems is no longer viable.

The change is taking place both at the level of technology and at the level of people. Table 12.1 shows the difference between thinking in a traditional, mechanistic world and in a systemic worldview, which is closer to or better reflects today's reality.

Table 12.1 Mechanistic versus systemic worldview

Mechanistic worldview	Systemic worldview
Objectivity, one truth, immutable laws	Construction of reality, many "truths," theses
Right, wrong; guilty, innocent	Contextuality, usefulness, connectivity
(Third-party) Control	Self-control, self-organization
Linear causal chains	Multiple interactions, feedback loops
Methods: Instruction, order, command, learning by trial and error	Methods: listening, questioning, dialogue, discussion, reflection, learning to learn
Roles: doers, leaders, and led, manipulation	Roles: impulse giver, gardener, enabler, development worker, coach
Formal logic, non-contradiction, exclusion	Integration of contradictions, inclusion
Hard facts, rational relationships	Integration of hard and soft factors (emotions, intuitions, communication processes)

What Does This Mean for IT and the Management of an IT Organization?

Take the new thinking of the DevOps approach as an example.

Following DevOps thought leader and "DevOps Cookbook" author Gene Kim, there are three ways to achieve DevOps. First, companies look at and optimize the IT value chain from requirements to IT operations. Second, there are feedback loops at all levels of the IT system – not just between developers and clients. In the third implementation strategy, stakeholders focus on continuous improvement, which they achieve through controlled experimentation.

In practice, it has proven successful to start with DevOps in an IT operations team and to take the processes automated there as the basis for development. However, the opposite approach, starting in development, can work just as well. For other newcomers, installing a pilot team to try out DevOps proves to be the best door opener into the agile IT world. Companies take the greatest possible risk when they immediately roll out the new IT value system to the entire organization. In that case, it is even more important to motivate, train, and educate their own professionals.

12.4 Digital Culture as the Foundation for a Modern IT Organization

An essential element for the digital transformation of companies is culture or, more specifically, the change in corporate culture.

In this context, one speaks of the creation of a digital culture. A culture as such is initially a very fuzzy entity. It is one of the so-called intangible assets that are often difficult to grasp, but are all the more important for the transformation of the company toward greater employee satisfaction and motivation. This cultural change also makes a significant contribution to greater customer satisfaction and customer loyalty.

But what exactly is behind this term and, above all, what can be the characteristics of such a digital culture?

- A new kind of collaboration through autonomous working conditions and collaboration.
- Openness and transparency.
- Agility and flexibility/entrepreneurship.
- Customer centricity.
- Learning and innovative spirit.
- Data-driven approach on the basis of which decisions are made.

On the way to such a digital culture, one thing is very important: Technology is only an enabler of such a culture! People are important in the process of change toward a digital culture. A culture of trust must be created, because trust and confidence as well as authenticity are the keys to a successful path through the transformation.

A big word of this time of change is "agility." In the context of digital culture, agility or an agile organization plays a big role because it reflects the nucleus of working. It is no longer stubborn specifications (command and control) and process-driven and highly structured work procedures from the Ford-Taylorism of assembly line work that are required today, but agile ways of working. What are the characteristics of organizations that have successfully introduced agile working?

- There is a culture of innovation and continuous learning.
- Flat hierarchies shape the cooperation.
- Changes in the market can be perceived at an early stage.
- The needs of constantly changing markets as well as their customers are continuously adapted.
- Opportunities in the market are recognized more quickly and thus market gaps are occupied efficiently.

How can this be implemented in everyday business? What is needed for the transformation?

A possible gap between employees and managers is an obstacle, e.g., in the form that managers still lead in the old command and control mode, but the employees have already reached another level and do not feel taken seriously by this management style. Consequently, this also leads to underperformance.

Therefore, it is important to recognize that culture change starts with leadership. Openness, transparency, and authenticity are not only important but crucial. In second the place, directly after leadership, comes the digital vision (LINK). Two further points are flexible working time models and the motto "Learning from mistakes – the fail-fast approach."

Finally, the four success factors that make digital culture a reality are:

1. *Leadership*: Define responsibilities for digitalization and the associated cultural change.
2. *Digital vision*: Formulate and constantly communicate a clear digitalization strategy and vision.
3. *Trust and authenticity*: Give employees trust and confidence and actively involve them in the change process.
4. *Agility and change leadership*: Opening a culture of continuous learning and innovation through change leaders.

References

1. *Schein, Edgar*: "Organizational Culture and Leadership", San Francisco: Jossey-Bass in Emmanuel Ogbonna (abridged from E. Ogbonna, Managing organisational culture: fantasy or reality, Human Resource Management Journal, 3, 2 (1993), pp. 42–54 in Jon Billsberry (ed.) The Effective Manager, Open University, Milton Keynes 1997).
2. *Malik, Fredmund*: Führen Leisten Leben, 6. Auflage, Campus Verlag, 2006.

Summary

Abstract

Not only the technological perspective of IT but more and more the human side of IT is coming into focus. IT drives change and must be able to handle great dynamics. This places high demands on the management of IT beyond any technology. Completely new skills and competencies are required. The purpose of this book is to make this clear, and the summary is intended to summarize this once again and bring it to the point.

From the historical development of the IT department with Plan-Build-Run to the current agile methods and forms of self-organization, the entire range of possible IT organizations was shown. What is the right role of IT in the company, and how must the CIO position himself accordingly? This is also one of the central topics in these very dynamically changing times. Finally, the relevant leadership tools for CIOs and IT managers were highlighted, which are so important for a successful transformation of the company in the digital age. This is an all-around look at all the topics that are important for the CIO and the management.

What should stick? From the author's perspective, seven characteristics are important for a true high-performance IT organization:

1. Clear results orientation and focus on business impact or value generation.
2. Do not think vertically in hierarchies, but act horizontally in value creation.
3. Innovative ability and creative drive.
4. CIO at board level and clear commitment from management.
5. Scalable architecture and cybersecurity.

V. Johanning, *Organization and Management of IT*,
https://doi.org/10.1007/978-3-658-39572-8_13

6. IT has a clear vision/objective.
7. Change leadership and talent management.

Finally, five golden rules for a successful IT organization will be established:

Rule 1: As little hierarchy as possible – process organization is "old school."
Rule 2: Agile and waterfall as a bimodal organization – Forget it! Everything is agile!
Rule 3: Everyone takes the lead!
Rule 4: The purpose and the target image are the foundation of a successful IT organization.
Rule 5: Establish credibility and create trust.

This leaves us with one thing to note: IT has become one of the key drivers of innovation and competitive strength for companies. The pure technology and service provider mentality is giving way to a role as a designer and innovator. The path from the traditional, hierarchical IT organization to the new world of agility, dynamics, change, and meaning and purpose must be found and taken. Therefore, the motto for all CIOs and IT managers is: Get going and move forward proactively instead of waiting for a long time like others do.

References

1. *Agarwal R., Sambamurthy V.*: "Principles and Models for organizing the IT-Function", MIS Quarterly Executive, Vol. 1, No. 1, March 2002.
2. *Beck, Kent et al.*: "Manifest für agile Softwareentwicklung," https://agilemanifesto.org/iso/de/manifesto.html, abgerufen am 29.12.2019.
3. *Brenner, Walter, Wulf Jochen, Winkler Till*: Organisationsgestaltung der Demand-IT", http://warhol.wiwi.hu-berlin.de/aigaion2/index.php/attachments/single/58, abgerufen am 14.04.2014.
4. *Detecon: Wolter Bernd, Chiesa Marco, Reich Christian*: IT-Organsiation 2015: Facelift oder Modellwechsel? (in Zusammenarbeit mit Bitkom), http://www.msm.uni-due.de/index.php?id=3335&no_cache=1&tx_eduext_pi4%5BshowUid%5D=2227&tx_eduext_pi4%5BspecialCMD%5D=download&tx_eduext_pi4%5Bfilename%5D=Detecon_ITOrga_2015.pdf, abgerufen am: 12.08.2014, Präsentation der Detecon Consulting von 05/2011.
5. *Fink, Franziska/Moeller, Michael*: "Purpose Driven Organizations", 1. Auflage, Schäffer Poeschel, 2018.
6. *Heinevetter, Thomas*: "IT-Organisation 2016: Faktor Mensch!", eine Studie von Kienbaum unter Kooperation von BITKOM, http://www.partnering.org/fileadmin/Event/BPC/2012/Vortr%C3%A4ge/Studie%20IT%20Organisation%202016%20-%20Faktor%20Mensch_Thomas%20Heinevetter_Kienbaum.pdf, abgerufen am 28.05.2014.
7. *Hierzer, Rupert*: "Prozessoptimierung 4.0: Den digitalen Wandel als Chance nutzen", 1. Auflage, Haufe, 2017.
8. *Johanning, Volker*: "IT-Strategie: Die IT für die digitale Transformation in der Industrie fit machen", 2. Auflage, Springer, 2019.
9. *Keese, Christoph*: "Silicon Valley: Was aus dem mächtigsten Tal der Welt auf uns zukommt", 4. Auflage, Knaus Verlag, 2014.
10. *Königswieser, Roswita, Hillebrand, Martin*: "Einführung in die systemische Organisationsberatung", 5. Auflage, Carl-Auer, 2015.
11. *Krüger, W.*: Organisation der Unternehmung, 3. Auflage, Verlag W. Kohlhammer, 1994.
12. *Laloux, Frederic*: "Reinventing Organizations: Ein Leitfaden zur Gestaltung sinnstiftender Formen der Zusammenarbeit", 1. Auflage, Verlag Franz Vahlen, 2015.
13. *Mohr, Günther*: "Systemische Organisationsanalyse", Verlag EHP, 2006.
14. *Pfläging, Nils*: Organisation für Komplexität, 1. Auflage, BoD – Books on Demand, 2013.

15. *Raitner, Marcus*: "Manifest für menschliche Führung: Sechs Thesen für neue Führung im Zeitalter der Digitalisierung", 1. Auflage, independently published, 2019.
16. *Schüller, Anne M., Steffen Alex T.*: "Die ORBIT-Organisation", 1. Auflage, GABAL, 2019.
17. *Wikipedia*: "TOGAF", https://de.wikipedia.org/wiki/TOGAF, abgerufen am 12.02.2020.
18. *Wunderer, Rolf*: Führung und Zusammenarbeit, Eine unternehmerische Führungslehre, 3. Auflage, Hermann Luchterhand Verlag, 2000.